P E A B O D Y
M U S E U M
C O L L E C T I O N S
S E R I E S

Gifts of the Great River

GIFTS OF THE GREAT RIVER

Arkansas Effigy Pottery from the Edwin Curtiss Collection

John H. House

Foreword by Ian W. Brown
Photographs by Hillel S. Burger
Rubie Watson, Series Editor

Peabody Museum Press, Harvard University

Editorial direction by Joan K. O'Donnell
Copy editing by Jane Kepp
Cover and text design by Kristina Kachele
Composition by Kristina Kachele
Color separations by iocolor, Seattle
Printed and bound in China by C&C Offset Printing Company, Ltd.

ISBN 0-87365-401-3

Library of Congress Cataloging-in-Publication Data:

House, John H.
Gifts of the great river : Arkansas effigy pottery from the Edwin Curtiss collection / John H. House ; foreword by Ian W. Brown ; photographs by Hillel S. Burger.
p. cm.—(Peabody Museum collections series)
Includes bibliographical references.
ISBN 0-87365-401-3 (pbk. : alk. paper)
1. Mississippian pottery—Collectors and collecting—Saint Francis River Valley (Mo. and Ark.)
2. Effigy pottery—Collectors and collecting—Saint Francis River Valley (Mo. and Ark.)
3. Indians of North America—Antiquities—Collection and preservation—Saint Francis River Valley (Mo. and Ark.) 4. Archaeological expeditions—Saint Francis River Valley (Mo. and Ark.)—History. 5. Saint Francis River Valley (Mo. and Ark.)—Antiquities.
6. Curtiss, Edwin—Journeys—Saint Francis River Valley (Mo. and Ark.) 7. Curtiss, Edwin—Archaeological collections. 8. Peabody Museum of Archaeology and Ethnology. I. Burger, Hillel. II. Peabody Museum of Archaeology and Ethnology. III. Title. IV. Series.

E98.M6815H68 2003
738.3'089'9707679—dc22
                              2003020973

∞ The paper used in this publication meets the minimum requirements of the American National Standard for Information Sciences—Permanence of Paper for Printed Library Materials, ANSI Z39.48-1984.

FRONTISPIECE: *Young Omaha, War Eagle, Little Missouri, and Pawnees,* by Charles Bird King, 1821. Portraits of American Indian warriors painted during the nineteenth century often show men with roached hair and the crowns of their heads painted red. The same features appear to be depicted on head vases from northeastern Arkansas dating to A.D. 1200–1600. Courtesy of Smithsonian American Art Museum, accession no. 1985.66.384,222, gift of Miss Helen Barlow.

Contents

Illustrations

PLATES

DISCOVERING THE CURTISS COLLECTION

Ian W. Brown

It gives me great pleasure to introduce John House's wonderful volume on Arkansas effigy pottery. I, too, have been involved with the pioneering archaeologist Edwin Curtiss, but from a somewhat different angle. In 1987, while curating the Hall of the North American Indian at the Peabody Museum, I happened to spend time in the storage annex examining collections from Tennessee. I remember coming to a shelf of human effigy vessels lined up all in a row, many of them with characteristic hunched backs and gaping holes in the backs of their heads. As a Southeastern archaeologist, I was familiar with such vessels, but I had never really looked at them closely. I was intrigued by the way some of them showed signs of having been made by the same potter. Tracking down site information in the catalogue, I was surprised to learn that almost all of these vessels had been collected by one industrious man, Edwin Curtiss.

Although Curtiss did most of his work for the Peabody in the Cumberland River region of Tennessee, John House demonstrates just how important Curtiss was as a supplier of Indian artifacts from other states. The race was on in the 1880s as newly formed museums across the land rushed to fill their coffers before there was nothing left. Curtiss, however, was no looter of ancient treasure. He kept quite detailed records for his day, on a par with the best of the other early archaeologists. Edward Palmer, another collector of Arkansas antiquities who is far better known than Curtiss, never matched the quality of Curtiss's descriptive notes. House offers enough examples of Curtiss's written observations to give readers a sense that Curtiss knew that the context of the find was just as important as the artifact. This understanding is remarkable considering that Curtiss was largely self-taught in archaeology.

Of course no real avenue for archaeological training existed when Curtiss began working for the Peabody Museum. In 1877 Frederic Ward Putnam, director of the museum, hired Curtiss to continue work that Putnam himself had begun in the vicinity of Nashville. Although most of Curtiss's efforts over the next four years were devoted to Tennessee, he also collected artifacts from Alabama, Kansas, Missouri, and Arkansas. Robert Mainfort and Sarah Demb, in their article "Edwin Curtiss's Archaeological Explorations along the St. Francis River, Northeast Arkansas, 1879–1880" (published in the journal *Arkansas Archeologist* in 2001), estimated that Curtiss contributed more than twenty-eight hundred artifacts to the Peabody's holdings during those four years. Although Curtiss worked in Arkansas for less than five months during the fall and winter of 1879–1880, he made the most of his time. A tireless digger, he calculated the weight of one shipment alone to Putnam at somewhere between twelve hundred and two thousand pounds.

Curtiss's focus on one specific region in Arkansas is part of what makes his work so valuable. With advice and encouragement from Putnam, he chose his field wisely. The St. Francis River region was, and still is, one of the greatest repositories of late prehistoric Native American artifacts in North America. It seems that virtually every Mississippian went to his or her grave accompanied by several well-made pots, and often these vessels are extraordinary examples of native craftsmanship. Why this region should stand out so distinctly for both the quality and the quantity of its ceramic effigy vessels remains an enigma. Most of the sites Curtiss excavated are now considered to be part of the late prehistoric–protohistoric Parkin phase. Scholars who have written about this phase and region over the years have made use of the magnificent collections at the Peabody Museum and have drawn liberally from Curtiss's notes, but no one has written a thorough description of the collection. House's work helps fills this void with regard to ceramics, especially effigy vessels.

Gifts of the Great River shows how much can be learned by studying museum collections with fresh eyes. The book is not only a worthy contribution to scholars but also a good read. It is about far more than pots. In his narrative, House visits the sites explored by Curtiss in the same order that Curtiss did, and once on location, he expands the story by providing a wealth of material relating to the sites in question and to the archaeologists who followed in Curtiss's footsteps. By elegantly weaving in background information on the local environment and on Native cultures, religion, and lore, House holds our interest and enriches our understanding. He brings his own experiences into the flow as well, allowing readers to share in the excitement and fascination of doing archaeology.

It was largely due to the achievements of Edwin Curtiss that the young Peabody Museum quickly became one of the finest repositories in the United States for Mississippian artifacts from the midcontinent. Putnam honored Curtiss after his death by displaying his whole collection in the "Moundbuilders" room as a memorial. The Peabody has continued to honor both Curtiss and the indigenous inhabitants of Arkansas with the publication of House's work. May there be many more such books!

ACKNOWLEDGMENTS

The research in the Peabody Museum collections on which this volume is based was carried out during visits to Cambridge, Massachusetts, in the summers of 2001 and 2002. I am grateful to Diana Loren, who facilitated my research in every way, and to Desirée Martinez, who assisted me in the museum annex in 2002. I am additionally grateful to Stephen LeBlanc, Amy Groleau, and Stuart Heebner for help during my research visits at the Peabody, to Hillel S. Burger for the color photographs in this volume, to Joan K. O'Donnell for her guidance as the Peabody Museum Press's editorial consultant, to Jane Kepp for her perceptive copy-editing, and to Kristina Kachele for the cover and text design for this book.

At the Arkansas Archeological Survey, I am particularly grateful to Jane Kellett for preparing many figures for this book. Numerous other Survey colleagues, in the midst of their busy professional lives, immediately set aside whatever they were doing to help me: Hester A. Davis, Lela Donat, Ann M. Early, Mary Farmer, Thomas J. Green, Jeffrey M. Mitchem, Timothy Mulvihill, and Leslie C. Stewart-Abernathy. At the

University of Arkansas Museum, Curator of Collections Mary Suter made comparative vessels available to me for study and helped me secure images for the figures on pages 25 and 34. Joseph C. Neal examined images of the bird effigy vessels in the Curtiss collection and suggested species identifications. Stephen Williams provided leads to research materials in the Peabody Museum archives and generously responded to my innumerable email queries with invaluable comments and advice. Others who generously shared data, provided me with research leads, or gave me much-appreciated comments and advice were James Cherry, Robert Dunnell, Gary Finnegan, Deborah House, April Layher, William Layher, John E. Miller III, Jon D. Muller, Kelly J. Mulvihill, Ruth Pasquine, Elizabeth Peña, Jeffrey Quilter, Mary Jo Schneider, Donald Slater, and Kevin Smith.

Gifts of the Great River

Edwin Curtiss's Pioneering Archaeological Explorations in Arkansas

In the late 1800s, during the first decades of the far-flung collecting expeditions sponsored by the Peabody Museum of American Archaeology and Ethnology (as it was then known), museum director Frederic Ward Putnam often hired nonprofessional fieldworkers to excavate sites for the museum. One of these was Edwin Curtiss, of Nashville, Tennessee. In 1879 and 1880, Curtiss traveled to the St. Francis River country of northeastern Arkansas, where he spent roughly eighty-six days in the field, at first working alone and later aided by "hands" whom he brought with him from Nashville. Archaeologists in Arkansas today regard Curtiss's work for the Peabody along the St. Francis as the first scientific archaeological excavation in their state.

Edwin Curtiss was born in North Lansing, New York, on January 27, 1830. Originally a tailor by trade, Curtiss joined the Commissary Department of the Union Army during the Civil War and served in Virginia and Tennessee, moving his family with him to the latter state. After the war Curtiss worked for the government as an independent contractor on levee, bridge, and railroad construction projects in various parts of the South and West. He may have been introduced to Frederic Ward Putnam by Gates P. Thruston, a noted antiquarian and subsequently author of *Antiquities of Tennessee and Adjacent States.* Like Curtiss, General Thruston had served in the Union army in Tennessee during the Civil War and had settled in Nashville afterward.[1] Curtiss collaborated in Putnam's excavations in Tennessee in 1877 and went into the field on his own, collecting antiquities for the Peabody Museum, in 1878–1880.[2]

Curtiss likely learned of the mounds and cemeteries of Arkansas's St. Francis country during his work on government jobs in that state. He set out for Arkansas in September 1879 after a short stay in Kansas City, where he had been working on a construction project and had also collected for the Peabody.

Along the St. Francis River in Arkansas, Curtiss and his associates excavated in at least seven ancient Indian sites. Their work secured for the Peabody Museum an enormous collection: nearly one thousand pottery vessels and hundreds of other specimens, including stone and bone tools, objects of copper and marine shell, bones of mammals, birds, and fish, charred corncobs, and human skeletal material. Importantly, Curtiss also sent back to Putnam, along with the objects themselves, a wealth of documentation. He included contextual data such as notes on graves and their contents and roughly drawn but highly informative maps of the sites and their settings.

Among the Curtiss collection vessels that have been housed at the Peabody for over a century are some sixty-nine effigy pots. Effigy pots are pottery vessels that were fashioned, in whole or in part, in the shape of a life form—everything from human heads and figures to complete fish and frogs and the heads of opossums, birds, and mythological creatures.

The effigies Curtiss collected in Arkansas all date from the late prehistoric era, preceding European contact—roughly A.D. 1200–1600. They came from cemeteries and mounds in Native American village sites in a small area along the winding St. Francis River in the Mississippi River lowlands. Archaeologists call the inhabitants of these archaeological sites—along with their contemporaries throughout much of the North American Southeast and Midwest—Mississippians. Collectively, the ancient

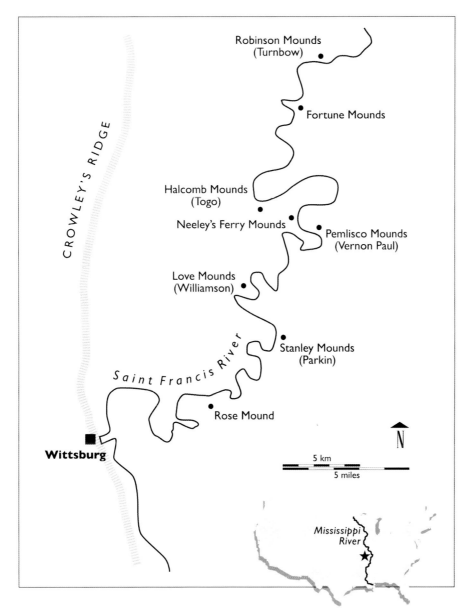

Sites excavated by Edwin Curtiss, 1879–1880. Map by Carol Cooperrider.

Robinson Mounds
(Turnbow)

Fortune Mounds

CROWLEY'S RIDGE

Halcomb Mounds
(Togo)

Neeley's Ferry Mounds

Pemlisco Mounds
(Vernon Paul)

Love Mounds
(Williamson)

Saint Francis River

Stanley Mounds
(Parkin)

Rose Mound

Wittsburg

N

5 km

5 miles

Mississippi
River

Mississippian Indians were forebears of Southeastern and Midwestern Indian tribes of the historic era and today. Archaeologists often refer to the local expression of late prehistoric Mississippian culture along the St. Francis River in northeastern Arkansas as the Parkin phase.[3]

Because much of Curtiss's Arkansas collection came from graves, the items fall within the purview of the Native American Graves Protection and Repatriation Act (NAGPRA) of 1990.[4] This law requires that institutions receiving federal support report all Native American human remains, funerary objects, and sacred objects or objects of cultural patrimony in their possession to pertinent, federally recognized Indian tribes. Under NAGPRA, a tribe that demonstrates lineal descent or cultural affiliation may take possession or otherwise determine the disposition of such objects. In compliance with the law, the Peabody Museum's staff spent much of the past decade developing the required information. The museum reported Native American human remains and grave goods from Arkansas to the Quapaw Tribe of Oklahoma, the Caddo Tribe of Oklahoma, and the Tunica–Biloxi Tribe of Louisiana.

This NAGPRA compliance effort included the first systematic inventory and description of the Curtiss collection and was the springboard for the research behind this book. At the annual meeting of the Society for American Archaeology in New Orleans in May 2001, Peabody curators Stephen LeBlanc and Diana Loren asked a group of archaeologists from the Arkansas Archeological Survey, a unit of the University of Arkansas system, to a luncheon meeting. There, they invited the Arkansas archaeologists to develop proposals for research and publication on the Curtiss collection. This invitation immediately spoke to my long–standing interest in Mississippian pottery effigies. With the support of the Peabody Museum and the Arkansas Archeological Survey, I made two research trips to Cambridge in 2001 and 2002 and, in collaboration with the Peabody's curators, photographer, and editorial consultant, prepared this volume.

This book is part of the continued unfolding of Edwin Curtiss's legacy. Curtiss's phenomenal harvest on the St. Francis River put the region on North American archaeologists' map for all time as an important place indeed. Generations of archae-ologists followed his footsteps to the region's mounds and village middens. They came initially for further collecting of objects from graves but later for groundbreaking explorations of Native American culture history and for anthropological research on the dynamics of human societies poised between foraging and intensive agriculture and between band or tribal organization and the archaic state.

Among the most important of Curtiss's successors was Clarence Bloomfield Moore, of the Academy of Natural Sciences of Philadelphia. Moore ascended the St. Francis in the winter of 1909–1910 in the steamboat *Gopher,* excavating more than fourteen hundred vessels from twenty-one sites, including many of the sites in which Curtiss had previously dug. Moore's 1910 article "Antiquities of the St. Francis, White and Black Rivers, Arkansas," lavishly illustrated with black and white photographs and color lithographs of artifacts, kept the region in the minds of collectors and scholars alike.[5] In this article, Moore published seven photographs of Curtiss collection vessels, made available to him by Putnam. This appears to be the earliest publication of items from Curtiss's Arkansas collection.

The University of Arkansas Museum's work in northeastern Arkansas is less well known. In the 1920s, the museum's director, Samuel C. Dellinger, became alarmed by what he perceived as the plundering of Arkansas's cultural heritage by both commercial diggers and out-of-state scientific institutions. Dellinger acquired a Carnegie Foundation grant of $20,000 and dispatched his students to excavate sites throughout Arkansas. One of these students, James Durham, supervised excavations at Neeley's Ferry and other sites in the Parkin area in 1933–1934, collecting at least eight hundred burials and more than nine hundred whole vessels. The pottery, housed at the University of Arkansas Museum–Arkansas Archeological Survey collection facility in Fayetteville, constitutes the most extensive collection of St. Francis River region vessels outside of Curtiss's materials in the Peabody.[6]

In the mid-twentieth century, the St. Francis region was among those explored by the Lower Mississippi Archaeological Survey, a collaboration among Harvard University's Peabody Museum, the School of Geology at Louisiana State University, and the Museum of Anthropology at the University of Michigan. This endeavor, often called "the Phillips, Ford, and Griffin survey" after its principal protagonists, Philip Phillips, James A. Ford, and James B. Griffin, set a new standard by focusing not on excavating graves and collecting whole vessels but on answering historical and anthropological questions.[7] North American archaeologists today regard the project as a landmark of innovation in archaeological survey methods.[8] The researchers of the Lower Mississippi Archaeological Survey viewed sites in their dynamic environmental settings and systematically explored variation in material culture across space and time. In the following pages I refer repeatedly to the Phillips, Ford, and Griffin survey and its resulting publication, *Archaeological Survey in the Lower Mississippi Alluvial Valley, 1940–1947* (1951 [2003]), as the baseline for current archaeological research in the St. Francis River region, both in the field and in the collections.

The huge collection that Curtiss made for Harvard, along with some collections resulting from mound explorations by the Smithsonian Institution a few years later,[9] served for decades as a prime source for characterizing the repertoires of early Indian ceramic artists, their themes, and their technical means.[10] Curtiss collection specimens were among the more than four thousand Mississippi Valley vessels photographed by Philip Phillips for his 1939 Harvard doctoral dissertation, "Introduction to the Archaeology of the Mississippi Valley."[11]

James B. Griffin incorporated many of Phillips's findings in his chapter "Distribution of Some Mississippi Period Vessel Shapes and Features" in the 1951 Phillips, Ford, and Griffin volume. In the section "Effigy Forms" and in the ensuing tables, Griffin formalized most of the terms and categories that I use in this book. He found that effigy pots had been collected from throughout the Mississippian world of the South and Midwest—and beyond. The majority of effigies, however, had come from the Lower Mississippi Archaeological Survey study area in northeastern Arkansas and adjacent southeastern Missouri, eastern Tennessee, and northeastern Mississippi, and in the Tennessee–Cumberland region centered on middle Tennessee. As he discussed the varied forms of effigy pottery—whole vessel effigies, rim effigies, serpent cats, head vases, fish bowls, and "effigy vessels of frog, opossum, and other beasts"—Griffin highlighted geographic variation in effigy forms and themes. In his pioneering analysis, Griffin ranged as far afield as the Florida Gulf Coast, the Southwestern United States, and Mesoamerica in placing the Mississippian effigies in context. He was intrigued by parallels between Mississippian effigy portrayals of humans and treatments of that theme by the prehistoric Casas Grandes people of what is now Chihuahua, Mexico. Many Curtiss collection vessels are among those illustrated in the photographic figures at the back of the 1951 *Survey* volume.

EARLY VISITORS to the lower Mississippi Valley left vivid accounts of traditional Indian pottery making that complement modern studies of archaeological ceramics. Writing at the beginning of the eighteenth century, French military engineer Dumont de Montigny observed that

> the industry of these Indian girls and women is admirable. I have already report–ed elsewhere with what skill, with their fingers alone and without a potter's wheel they make all sorts of pottery.
>
> After having gathered the earth suitable for this kind of work, and having well cleaned it, they take shells which they grind and reduce to a very fine powder; they mix this very fine dust with the earth which they have provided, and, mois–tening the whole with a little water, they knead it with the hands and feet, forming a dough of which they make rolls 6 or 7 feet long and of whatever thickness is desired. Should they wish to fashion a dish or a vessel, they take one of these rolls and, holding down one end with the thumb of the left hand they turn it around with admirable swiftness and dexterity, describing a spiral; from time to time they dip their fingers in water, which they are always careful to have near them, and with the right hand they smooth the inside and outside of the vessel they intend to form, which, without this care, would be undulated.
>
> In this manner they make all sorts of utensils of earth, dishes, plates, pans, pots, and pitchers, some of which contain 40 and 50 pints. The baking of this pottery does not cause them much trouble. After having dried it in the shade they build a great fire, and when they think they have enough coals they clear a place in the middle where they arrange the vessels and cover them with the coals.[12]

Modern laboratory studies help us fill out this sketch of the technical means avail–able to Mississippian potters and their use of those means in creating effigy pottery.[13]

The Indian ceramic artists of the St. Francis River could have obtained their materials from their immediate environment. The low-lying backswamps behind their villages would have provided clays from sediments deposited more than three thousand years earlier, when the Mississippi River flowed in the westernmost of its Holocene channels. These clays contain large proportions of unweathered clay minerals such as illite that cause wet clay to shrink markedly as it dries. Indian potters met the challenge of making pots that would not crack and fall apart as they dried by adding material known as "temper." Temper made of pulverized, burned river mussel shell is the hallmark of Mississippian ceramics. River mussel shells are perennially abundant in the St. Francis River. In the nineteenth century, river mussel shells were harvested to be cut into circular blanks for "pearl" buttons. Today they are harvested to manufacture cores for cultured pearls. Experimentation, along with technical studies of archaeological ceramics, indicates that the proportion by volume of shell temper in a prehistoric Mississippian pot can be as high as 50 percent.

Many of the formally simpler effigies illustrated in this book were manufactured from the comparatively coarse shell-tempered paste that archaeologists often refer to as "Neeley's Ferry paste." The more intricately sculpted examples were made from a fine-textured shell-tempered paste known as "Bell paste," which in most cases also contains "grog"—pulverized fired clay or potsherds—although this is difficult to observe without microscopic examination of a fresh fracture. Not surprisingly, experimenters have demonstrated that coarse shell-tempered ware is comparatively resistant to the kind of "thermal shock" that cooking pots undergo, whereas the finer-textured Bell paste can be more readily molded and sculpted.

The geographical distribution of vessels made from these two kinds of paste is surely bound up in historical contingencies as well as technology and function. Exploring the St. Francis region in 1910, Moore lamented the "general inferiority" of St. Francis River pottery, which partly reflected the preponderance of coarse shell-tempered ware. A few decades later, Phillips, Ford, and Griffin remarked on the higher frequencies of sherds in Bell paste in what they called the Memphis subarea, along the Mississippi, in comparison with higher frequencies of Neeley's Ferry paste at sites of the interior St. Francis subarea (corresponding to what came to be called the

Parkin phase). They believed this distribution supported their argument that the two areas were inhabited by culturally distinct societies.

We know little yet about how, once they had prepared the clay, Mississippian potters built their vessels. Notwithstanding mention of coil building in historical accounts, one rarely observes fractures along coil lines in archaeological specimens. There is some evidence that potters used previously fashioned bowls as molds for forming portions of new vessels. Use of a paddle–and–anvil technique to compact and thin vessel walls, whether they were coiled or not, may be seen in the somewhat faceted character of the walls of archaeological vessels.[14]

John E. Miller III, an archaeologist with the Arkansas Highway and Transportation Department, has experimented extensively with replicating Native American pottery from Arkansas. In January 2002 he joined me in making replicas of two of the rim effigies in the Curtiss collection using shell–tempered native clay. Rim effigies are

John E. Miller III attaches a head and neck assembly to a replica of the Peabody's cat-serpent bowl (80-20-10/21621; pl. 21). Courtesy Arkansas Archeological Survey; photograph by John H. House.

bowls or jars to which potters attached appendages such as heads and tails to the vessel rim (see, for example, pl. 3). We found it effective, after forming the vessel, to model the effigy appendages separately from very plastic clay and then weld or press them onto the correspondingly still plastic clay of the vessel body. Many rim effigies exhibit bulges in the surface contour at the juncture between the neck of the effigy figure and the rim of the vessel, inside and out (see pl. 4 for an example). These bulges appear to consist of clay applied to strengthen the juncture and buttress the rim against the weight of the effigy head while the vessel dried. Whatever techniques the ancient potters used to attach heads and tails to rims, they were quite effective; archaeological vessels rarely exhibit breaks across these junctures.

Effigies are often so thoroughly worked that they leave few clues to the sequence of rolling, cutting, bending, and pinching used to create the finished forms. In some instances, however, abrupt changes in surface contours appear to distinguish the components from which the effigies were assembled.

One modeling technique that appears widely, though not frequently, in Mississippian effigies is *fenestration*—the creation of openings, or "windows," through modeled forms. Some instances of fenestration are merely negative spaces left by the rendering of life forms three-dimensionally. In fenestrations through head crests or tail plumage, however, the intent more likely was to add to the visual content of the object.

Beyond the modeling of effigy components, we can identify a number of additional techniques the artisans who made the Curtiss effigies employed for manipulating clay. They *appliquéd* fillets—strips of clay—to render limbs, and they appliquéd nodes—pellets of clay—to render eyes. Sometimes they accentuated such appliquéd elements by *excising,* or removing, some areas of surface to leave other areas in relief. They used *punctation,* the punching of holes with implements of a variety of sizes and shapes, to render pupils of eyes. Linear or graphic elements were sometimes added to three-dimensional forms. *Incision* refers to drawing lines with a pointed implement in soft clay. Archaeologists use the term "wet-paste incision" to refer to an incision executed when the clay was still plastic, leaving raised ridges, or "burrs," where the clay was pushed aside by the incising tool. Alternatively, graphic elements could be added after

John E. Miller III incises a mouth design on the replica of the cat-serpent bowl (80-20-10/21621; pl. 21). Courtesy Arkansas Archeological Survey; photograph by John H. House.

the vessel dried. This is referred to as *engraving;* it results in fine lines with a jagged, scratchy character.

As a final step before drying, vessels could be *polished.* At Mississippian habitation sites, archaeologists find pebbles of hard, fine-grained rock bearing lustrous areas. These were evidently used as pottery polishing stones.[15] Potters used such stones to produce smooth, shiny vessel surfaces that in fact consist of myriad tiny, elongated, polished facets.

Archaeologists have never found kilns or concentrations of sherds from vessels damaged in manufacturing in Mississippian sites. This implies that potters fired their vessels in open places away from dwellings. Experimentation suggests that Mississippian vessels were fired at temperatures in the range of 550° to 750° C.

Early historic accounts from the width and breadth of the Southeast refer predominantly, if not exclusively, to women as having been the potters.[16] The artistry embodied by effigy vessels raises interesting questions about gender in prehistoric Mississippian art. Did a dichotomy exist between masculine art styles, as represented in engraved shell, stone, and sheet copper, and feminine styles, as seen in pottery? Most visual elements of Mississippian effigies were created at the time the vessel was being fashioned and the clay was still plastic, which would tend to implicate women artists. Some scholars, however, have seen complex engraved designs on Mississippian ceramics—produced by a technique that could have been "postponed" until after the vessel had dried or even been fired—as having stylistic affinities to the "masculine" media.[17]

"This Is the Place
We Have Long Sought"

On the morning of September 25, 1879, Edwin Curtiss arrived in Little Rock, Arkansas, after a two-day train journey from St. Louis. A few days later, he made a short trip to the vicinity of Conway, about thirty miles to the northwest, where he "explored two mounds and got some fine pottery 8 pieces."

Curtiss appears to have delayed his departure for the St. Francis River country because of a yellow fever quarantine imposed by the Little Rock and Arkansas State Boards of Health. During his stay in Little Rock, Curtiss visited the nearby Toltec, or Knapp, Mounds, where he did some digging and recorded some observations that he sent to Putnam, accompanied by a sketch map of the site.[18] Writing to Putnam on the eve of his departure from Little Rock, Curtiss anticipated a sojourn in a wild country where he would be obliged to "eat corn or . . . ho[e] cake and hog meat and drink there black coffee" but would be happy if he could "find good things."

The quarantine having been lifted, Curtiss left for northeastern Arkansas at the end of October. From Little Rock, he traveled by way of the new Memphis and Little Rock

Railroad to within thirty-six miles of Memphis and thence to the river port of Wittsburg, his jumping-off place for the St. Francis River country.

At the close of his first week in the field, Curtiss wrote Putnam that he had already obtained a larger collection than he had ever before found at one place. The St. Francis River country was as wild and rugged as he had expected: "This is certainly a wild country[.] we have a serenade every night of the wolves and not infrequently the scream of the panther is he[a]rd in the woods after night[.] night before last night the lady at the farm where I am stopping had a large hog killed by the bears and eaten by them[.] but this is the place we have long sought[.]" Because he had found it difficult to hire local labor or secure meals and lodging near the places where he had to work, Curtiss wrote Putnam that he intended to bring in his own camping gear and "old hands" from Nashville. Curtiss's correspondence with Putnam includes references to buying vessels that had been collected by people working at one site while Curtiss was working on another. This hints that Curtiss sometimes compensated his "hands" with payments by the vessel instead of by a daily wage.

Curtiss began his work in eastern Arkansas's St. Francis River country at Stanly Mounds. The precise location of the Stanly Mounds had been lost for a century until Phyllis Morse, of the Arkansas Archeological Survey, found in the tax records at the Cross County Courthouse that in 1879 John Stanley had owned the forty acres encompassing the Parkin archaeological site.[19] Today the Parkin site is in an Arkansas State Park on the outskirts of the small town of Parkin. Walking out on the site from the museum, visitors see the elevated village area, which encompassed seventeen acres, and can trace the ditches, or moat, that once enclosed the village on three sides. The twenty-seven-foot-high principal mound rises against the tree line on the river-bank beyond the village area. Jeffrey M. Mitchem, the Arkansas Archeological Survey's station archaeologist for the Parkin site, has directed excavations there since 1991. Mitchem and his team have found the village deposit, up to 1.2 meters deep, to consist of intricate sequences of fills, house floors, construction debris, and graves.

The town of Parkin, which grew up beside the railroad and a wood products mill in the late 1800s, is today an economically depressed Arkansas Delta town with high unemployment and empty businesses lining Main Street. The scene was livelier in the

The Parkin site today, looking west across the village area toward the principal mound, with the moat in the foreground. Courtesy Arkansas Archeological Survey; photograph by Timothy Mulvihill.

summer of 1965, when, during my high–school years, I participated in the University of Arkansas Museum–Arkansas Archeological Society training session at Parkin. This was in the waning days of the tenant farmer era and at the high tide of the great migration of African Americans to the cities of the North. I remember the hot twilight on Main Street on the evenings when University of Arkansas Museum director Charles R. McGimsey presented lectures in City Hall. In a festive atmosphere, farm families thronged the sidewalks, greeting one another while doing their Friday night shopping in a Chinese grocery store. Dusty pickup trucks lined the street, their beds full of small children.

Residents of Parkin then and now might be surprised to learn of scholars' long-standing interest in the ancient village mound north of town. In the 1940s and '50s, the Parkin site and other sites along that stretch of the St. Francis River played a pivotal role in the development of American archaeological methods. Analyzing and comparing pottery sherd collections from the width and breadth of the lower Mississippi survey area, James B. Griffin was struck by the distinctiveness of pottery samples from sites in the St. Francis River region. He found that pottery to contrast with pottery from contemporaneous sites bordering the Mississippi River to the east. By the early 1950s, the "St. Francis focus"—later renamed the "Parkin phase"—had become an exemplar of the potential for correlating constellations of archaeological sites with specific past societies.[20] In later decades, archaeologists saw the Parkin site and its evident satellite villages as the embodiment of a prehistoric "chiefdom," a theorized social form characterized by centralized leadership of a large, multicommunity territory.[21]

The Parkin archaeological site may be the town of Casqui visited by the *entrada,* or expedition, of Hernando de Soto in June 1541. The Spaniards arrived in the paramount town of the province of Casqui after emerging from what the anonymous Gentleman of Elvas, a survivor of the expedition and one of its principal chroniclers, termed "the worst tract for swamps and water that they had found in all Florida." At Casqui, the chroniclers described four hundred houses within a palisade and a large mound on which the Spaniards erected a wooden cross.[22] Glass chevron beads and brass hawksbells found at the Parkin site may be vestiges of the sixteenth-century Spanish *entrada.*

With the recognition that Curtiss's Stanly Mounds and Parkin are the same site, we can see that Curtiss's map corresponds well with a modern topographic map of Parkin (see pp. 20 and 21). Curtiss found some twenty mounds on eighteen acres surrounded on three sides by a deep ditch that held water most of the year. He excavated graves in three of the smaller mounds. On his sketch map, he filled in the outlines of those mounds and designated each by number. No obvious vestiges of these small mounds exist today. Curtiss commented on the prevalence of "what the inhabitants calls brick" (fired clay daub from the walls or roof interiors of burned structures), the richness of the graves in pottery and other artifacts, and the good preservation of the skeletons. In the first of the mounds he dug at Parkin, Curtiss reported finding "not an adult . . . all children or young people . . . and all wealthy, for there was something found in evry one." Today, the Peabody Museum has 162 catalogued objects collected by Curtiss at Stanly Mounds, including pottery vessels, marine shell beads, tools of bone and antler, and ground stone celts (ungrooved axes).

Among the five effigies that Curtiss found at Stanly Mounds were a small frog effigy jar (pl. 1) and a conch shell effigy cup painted red and white (pl. 2). Museum visitors today delight in the bright colors of Mississippian painted vessels, and one assumes that the Indians who made and used the vessels delighted in them as well. Archaeologists recognize all–over red treatments, red and white treatments, and polychrome treatments that exhibit, in interstices between red and white elements, vestiges of a black pigment that is perhaps organic. Sophisticated chemical analyses support long–standing opinions that the red mineral pigment is iron based, presumably hematite or red ocher, whereas the white pigment is rich in aluminum and is probably kaolin. Both minerals occur in the uplands bordering the Mississippi River flood-plain. The presence of aluminum and silicon, the elemental signature of clay, in even the red paint samples supports the assumption that potters applied the pigments to the vessels as slips, or suspensions of clay and mineral pigment.[23]

REFERRING TO Stanly Mounds in a letter to Putnam, Curtiss wrote that "in 1867 in the big overflow there were thousands of stock fetched here to get out of the water and they broke a great deal of pottery tromping it." Flooding is a recurrent theme in Curtiss's St. Francis River narratives. Though the Mississippi River runs more than twenty–five miles to the east, all of the sites Curtiss excavated lay within the Mississippi's floodplain before construction of the modern levee system in the decades following his explorations. As Egypt and its distinctive ancient civilization were gifts of the Nile, so the Mississippi Delta country and its prehistoric Indian cultures were gifts of the stream that Algonquian–speaking Indians called the Great River. The Mississippi, in its floods and restless channel movements, created the region's highly varied landforms—and cyclically erased them to begin anew.

These varied landforms include glacial outwash deposits on high terraces, insular upland remnants mantled with windlaid silt (loess), and belts of complex meander topography interspersed with backswamps. Between four thousand and six thousand years ago the Mississippi flowed against its western valley wall at the foot of Crowleys Ridge (a hilly, two–hundred–mile–long upland remnant). There, over the millennia, the river's floods laid down a vast deposit of sandy and loamy sediments forming an

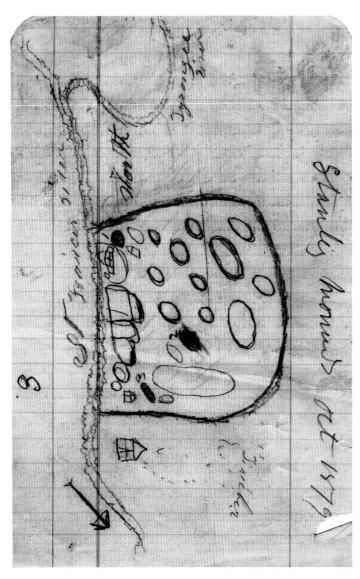

Curtiss's sketch map of Stanly Mounds (Parkin), oriented with north at top. Accession file 80-20, Peabody Museum Archives, Harvard University.

elevated ridge several miles wide, its surface intricately scrolled with channel scars, loamy natural levees, and corresponding, arcing sandy point bar ridges marking successive beach lines. After the Mississippi River shifted eastward, the comparatively miniscule flow of the St. Francis River, derived from Ozark headwaters, came to occupy the sinuous, Mississippi-sized channel of the former river.[24]

Indians settled on these high alluvial landforms along the banks of lakes filling old Mississippi channel scars and along the network of rivers and bayous interconnecting them. The phenomenal fertility of the alluvial soils supported both bountiful natural ecosystems and the maize-beans-and-squash horticulture of the Mississippians.

Flooding perennially dominated the landscape. Every spring for thousands of years, the snowmelt of the Rocky Mountains, the northern Great Plains, the upper Midwest, and the eastern flank of the Appalachians swelled the Mississippi and sent its brown waters over the river's banks south of modern-day New Madrid, Missouri, and into the vast interior flood basin to the west. The floodwaters gathered there in the Pemiscot Bayou, in the Little River, with its Left Hand and Right Hand Chutes, and in the Tyronza River and made their way to the St. Francis. There they met Mississippi water backing up the St. Francis from its mouth far to the

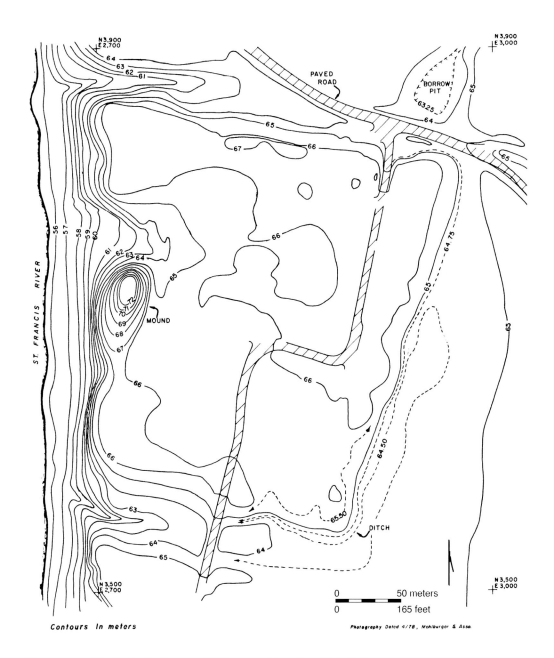

Modern map of the Parkin site. Courtesy Mehlberger and Associates, Little Rock.

21

south, near Helena, Arkansas. In years of abundant snowmelt, water overfilled the swamps between the high alluvium along the St. Francis and the high alluvium along the Mississippi. It then crept silently out of the woods and cane brakes until it topped the highest alluvial ridges, where the Indians had built their villages.

Flooding brought hardship to human communities, but it also rejuvenated the fertility of the soils and refilled the lakes, bayous, and wooded backswamps with nutrient-rich water. The waters teemed with fish, turtles, and other aquatic life.[25] Forests harbored white-tailed deer, raccoons, opossums, and other terrestrial species that provided meat, hides, and fur. Autumn and winter brought flights of ducks and other waterfowl to dive in the open waters or dabble for acorns in the flooded forests. Curtiss was the first of many archaeologists to note the abundance of animal and fish bones in prehistoric village middens.[26] Moreover, the network of waterways connected communities with each other and with the wider world as Indians plied them in wooden dugout canoes.

Curtiss completed his work at Stanly Mounds in mid-November 1879 and proceeded to Memphis to ship his collection to Putnam at the Peabody. From there he paid a visit to Nashville. He wrote Putnam from Nashville that he had cut short his stay in Memphis because of the persistence of "cases," presumably of yellow fever, in that city. In Nashville, Curtiss recruited two of his "old hands" to assist him in his Arkansas labors.

Curtiss's correspondence with Putnam during the period of his fieldwork in Arkansas includes instructions to Putnam to send money to his wife, who, for most of this time, was "stopping" at Great Bend Village, Susquehanna County, Pennsylvania. According to the 1870 United States census and the later Davidson County, Tennessee, census, Curtiss's wife was named Eliza (probably Elizabeth). They had a daughter, Carrie Curtis (unlike her father, she spelled her name with one *s*).[27]

Curtiss resumed his work in Arkansas in mid-December at Neeley's Ferry, on the west bank of the St. Francis River five miles above Stanly Mounds. Curtiss's sketch map of the Neeley's Ferry site and its environs shows, at the site itself, a curving slough or ditch enclosing a large mound and other features, evidently including two cabins. Three days before Christmas, Curtiss wrote Putnam that at Neeley's Ferry he had found a mound eight feet high that "had never been ploughed and was as the Natives had left it." He dug in this large mound and in other portions of the site, collecting some 353 objects that are now catalogued in the Peabody Museum. They include pottery vessels, marine shell beads, tools of bone and antler, lumps of mineral pigment, charred corncobs, discoidal stones used in a game called *chunkey*,[28] a wolf skull, and ground stone celts.

Among the thirty whole or fragmentary effigies that Curtiss excavated at Neeley's Ferry, rim effigy vessels are particularly conspicuous. Rim effigy bowls, which perhaps had prototypes in carved wooden bowls, are one of the most consistently occurring and geographically widespread of Mississippian artifact types.[29] The simplest rim effigy bowls have a head rising from the rim on one side, and opposite it, an appendage rendering a more-or-less stylized tail. Common elaborations of this theme are small tabs at the rim representing limbs, as well as appliquéd strips on the bowl exterior representing limbs or wings with feathers. Pervasive wear on the heads of some rim effigy bowls suggests that the heads served as handles.

Birds were the life form most frequently represented on rim effigies at Neeley's

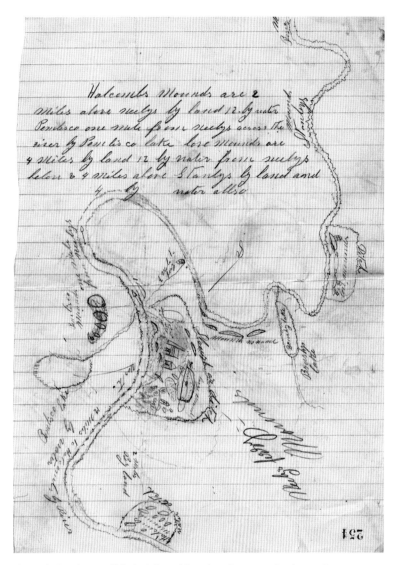

Curtiss's sketch map of Neeley's Ferry Mounds and environs. South is at the top. Accession file 80-20, Peabody Museum Archives, Harvard University.

The principal mound at the Neeley's Ferry site at the time of the University of Arkansas Museum's excavations in 1933. Courtesy University of Arkansas Museum.

Ferry and other St. Francis River sites. In the northeastern Arkansas archaeological collections at the University of Arkansas Museum in Fayetteville, ornithologist Joseph C. Neal has identified 115 bird effigies. Many of these were collected during the University of Arkansas Museum's excavations at Mississippian sites along the St. Francis River during the 1930s. Neal observed that the artists in many cases rendered the species "field marks" that are familiar to birders today. Among the species he found represented in the museum's effigies were swan, goose, wood duck, hooded merganser, wild turkey, vulture, owl, and a bird representing either the prairie chicken, the grouse, or the bobwhite. Neal also noted the presence of facial markings characteristic of falcons on representations of composite or mythological creatures.[30]

Curtiss worked at Neeley's Ferry into late January 1880. During this time he excavated briefly at the Pemlisco Mounds across the river from Neeley's Ferry. "I explored among them with one man for one day and found nothing to encourage me so I left there," he wrote. Today this site is known as Vernon Paul. The University of Arkansas

Museum excavated at Vernon Paul in 1933, collecting a large number of vessels. One of these, illustrated above, shares many features with a Curtiss vessel from Neeley's Ferry (pl. 9) but exhibits a three-dimensional panther figure on the tail tab.

ON THE TWENTY-FOURTH of January, Curtiss wrote Putnam from Memphis as he prepared to ship to the museum "over three hundred pieces of pottery and some very large ones and I think 15 cranias, 6 pipes or more and some very beautiful things." Curtiss informed Putnam that he had five men at work because he wanted to complete the excavations on the St. Francis before the arrival of hot weather. He continued, "It is certainly one of the most wonderful places that I have ever been in for the works are vast and numerous and I can fill the museum in one year if you so desire."

In 1910, Clarence B. Moore followed Curtiss's lead to Neeley's Ferry, then known as the Starwood Place, and excavated 95 graves and 175 pottery vessels, along with other items.[31] The University of Arkansas Museum followed two decades later, excavating 81 graves and collecting 111 ceramic vessels.[32] Most recently, in June 1996, the Arkansas Archeological Society returned to the banks of the St. Francis River for its annual training session, conducting five and a half days of work at Neeley's Ferry. The team excavated portions of a burned structure on the plowed-down remnant of the principal remaining mound and explored an area of expected fortifications on the northern edge of the site.[33]

From Curtiss's time to the present, archaeologists have been awestruck by the sheer magnitude of the Mississippian village middens of the St. Francis River area. In a section titled "Analysis of Occupation Site Plans" in the 1951 *Survey* volume, James A. Ford placed Parkin (Curtiss's Stanly Mounds), Fortune Mounds, and Rose Mound among the most developed examples of the "St. Francis–type" site category, which he characterized as "Large Rectangular Village Sites with Temple Mounds." It was evident to Ford that these were "places where fairly large numbers of people lived and the ceremonial center, the plaza with its surrounding mounds, has become the center of a town." He continued: "The concentration of refuse in a rectangular area surrounded by a ditch indicates almost conclusively that these towns were fortified. A stockade as well as a ditch probably protected as well as defined the village area."[34]

Elsewhere in the *Survey* volume, the authors found the presence of numerous large villages or town sites in a small area along the St. Francis River reminiscent of the sixteenth-century landscape described by the chroniclers of the de Soto entrada. Of the Province of Casqui, the Gentleman of Elvas wrote, "The land is higher, drier, and more fertile than any other along the river that had been seen until then . . . the greater part of the way lying through fields thickly set with great towns, two or three of them to be seen from one."[35]

At Parkin, Jeffrey M. Mitchem and his co-workers are beginning to fill in the outlines of life in these populous prehistoric Indian towns.[36] They have found that the Natives lived in houses that were almost exactly four meters square. Lines of vertical posts set in the ground formed the walls, which in turn supported a trussed, pitched roof covered with thatch. The walls appear to have been covered with woven cane mats lashed to the vertical posts. To his surprise, Mitchem found no evidence that the walls of houses at Parkin were "daubed," that is, covered with clay plaster. The ubiquitous burned clay debris in the midden appears to have come mainly from clay plaster applied to the interior of the roof as fireproofing around a smoke hole. The houses were floored with prepared clay surfaces and typically had a clay-lined hearth in the center of the floor. Also in the interiors of houses were evident smudge pits containing charred corncobs. One pictures the Indians passing the warm months of the year in the hanging smoke of slow-burning corncobs that kept away the clouds of ravenous, humming mosquitoes.

We know nothing about the spacing of houses or the arrangement of houses within villages in the Parkin phase. In nearby areas, however, archaeologists have exposed, just below the plow zone, whole villages with foundations of houses in orderly rows flanking courtyards and small plazas.[37] Every household no doubt had a granary. The granaries may have been like those the missionary Gravier saw among the Tunica people at the turn of the eighteenth century. He described them as "made like dovecotes, built on four large posts, 15 or 16 feet high, well put together and well polished, so that the mice cannot climb up. In this way they protect their corn and squashes."[38] At a larger scale, the villages appear to have been laid out around central plazas flanked by a mound or mounds.

Curtiss's maps from 1879–1880 help us to appreciate that there were once numerous mounds at these sites of which no traces remain today. Some of these were burial mounds. At Parkin, Curtiss dug in three mounds (of the twenty-one smaller mounds then extant) and struck numerous graves. Moore observed in 1910 that "the Parkin Mound, similar in type to the Rose Mound, has a great upper surface, as a rule flat, on which are many humps and rises."[39] Other mounds were platforms for structures. The six-meter-high mound on the west side of the Parkin site has an upper platform and a lower platform, or apron. Excavations on the upper platform in 1965 and 1966 revealed fills from successive episodes of mound building alternating with layers of habitation debris and stubs of charred posts.[40] Several superimposed house floors were found in an excavation on the apron of the mound.[41]

Archaeologists of Curtiss's and Moore's generations were drawn to the large town sites along the St. Francis River because they were also cemeteries containing pottery vessels and other grave goods. At Parkin, graves have been found throughout the site, often close to houses. Thousands of people, representing generations of Native Americans, were buried in sites like Parkin and Neeley's Ferry.

Ford inferred that the deep archaeological deposits in St. Francis–type sites were largely accumulations of habitation debris in areas enclosed by former palisades. We have learned since that the depth of these sites typically resulted from episodes of deliberate filling on top of former house sites, followed by construction of more houses, followed by more filling, and so forth, until the entire village site became a "mound" as much as two meters high.

In this portion of the Southeast, the Spanish chroniclers portrayed warlike societies and large towns defended by palisades and moats. Notwithstanding, archaeologists have found it difficult to identify traces of palisades. At Parkin, Mitchem and his co-workers found a line of posts and a portion of a possible bastion on the east edge of the village, at the crest of the slope up from the evident moat. The trench excavated in 1996 on the north edge of Neeley's Ferry revealed a moat measuring fourteen meters wide and extending one meter deep from the present ground surface. This presumably corresponds to the enclosing "ditch or slough" that Curtiss indicated on his sketch map (see p. 23). On the crest of the slope just within the ditch, the 1996 excavators found a line of post holes averaging twenty-one centimeters in diameter and spaced an average of thirty-four centimeters apart.[42]

CURTISS WROTE to Putnam from Memphis in late January 1880, declaring that he intended to "move up to the Fortune Mounds . . . which if one half is true I shall get many interesting things there and a large quandity." When he wrote Putnam again, it was the second of February and he was sitting in a tent at Fortune Mounds. "The weather is bad cold and it is snowing, blowing and the fire sends most of the smoke in the tent and it is hard on the eyes."

Prefacing his account with the words, "This Fortune place is another wonder," Curtiss exulted in the discovery of a naturalistic head vase, which has become the most celebrated artifact among the Curtiss materials in the Peabody (pl. 15). The previous day, two of his "old hands" (later identified as Joe Woods and George Woods) had found six vessels, which, they told Curtiss, they were making a present of to

Putnam. "One in particular is a vessel in the shape of a man's head and as large with ears as perfect, one on and the other could not be found[,] but the one that is on cannot be excelled by any artist of today. Even the eyes are in the sightless [illegible] the nose and the mouth teeth and all are perfect and is of itself a wonder."

Examining this head vase was the high point of my second research visit to the Peabody Museum. Arriving in the curators' workroom just off the second-floor landing a few minutes after nine o'clock one morning, I waited as Diana Loren went to the vault. She returned with the "wonder" that Curtiss's co-workers had taken from the earth at Fortune on that winter day over a century ago. I pulled on latex gloves and spent the next three hours making notes about this remarkable artifact.

After the naturalistic proportions of the face, I was most struck by the marked slant of the facial plane, a feature that suggested to me that the artist intended the face to be viewed from an elevated angle. A raised, teardrop-shaped element extends from the top of the forehead to the middle of the back of the head, encompassing the flaring neck of the vessel; this may represent the man's roached hair arrangement. Similarly, the thick, dark red slip on the surface between the "roach" and the border of the face appears to show red paint on the shaven crown of the head, much like that depicted on the heads of warriors in nineteenth-century North American Indian portraits (see frontispiece). The pale buff slip on the face is difficult to distinguish from the oxidized underlying paste of the vessel wall. Traces of orange streaking on the edge of the face—where the red slip appears to have been accidentally mixed with the buff— evoked, for me, the moment of the artwork's creation.

Diana rejoined me at the end of the morning, bringing a small flashlight. She directed the light down the mouth of the vessel, and we could see that the vessel wall itself had been formed to approximate the contours of a human face; most notably, the eye sockets were inset. The detailed features—nose, lips, brow ridges—had then been modeled from applied strips of clay and finished by incising and punctation. The artist had defined the outlines of the open eyes with bold incised arcs, leaving the eyes blank ("sightless"), without pupils.

Head vases from eastern Arkansas have excited interest and admiration since they were first reported in the late nineteenth century. "Classic" head vases, broadly in the

Design on an engraved marine shell gorget from the McDuffee site, Craighead County, Arkansas. Note the forelock ornaments. Courtesy University of Arkansas Museum; artwork by Linda Murphy.

style of the Fortune example, occur in northeastern Arkansas and the adjacent Missouri boot heel.[43] A few additional head vases, in divergent styles, have been found in the Cairo Lowland region of southeastern Missouri and Kentucky and along the lower Arkansas River in the vicinity of Little Rock and below.

In his discussion of effigies in the 1951 *Survey* volume, James B. Griffin enumerated the typical characteristics of eastern Arkansas head vases. They are almost always painted red and white or buff. The vessel opening is at the top of the head. The ears have several perforations, and the mouth is depicted partly open, exposing the teeth. There is a perforation at the midline of the face at the hairline, usually in a small knob. This perforation was probably for the attachment of forelock beads like those frequently depicted in Mississippian shell art. An example is the McDuffee gorget from Craighead County, Arkansas, a short distance northwest from the scene of Curtiss's 1879–1880 excavations.

Although the facial proportions and placement of features on the Peabody Museum's Fortune Mounds head vase and a few other examples are naturalistic, a greater number of head vases exhibit a stylized wide face. Many head vases bear incised patterns on the face; these are usually interpreted as depicting tattoos or scarification. Like the Fortune Mounds head vase, many others exhibit a raised, teardrop-shaped element extending from the crown to the back of the head, possibly depicting a roached hair arrangement. Some head vases have a short pedestal base or neck.

Despite the naturalism of some examples, it is unlikely that head vases were portraits of individual persons, as were, arguably, the Moche vessels of Peru that often naturalistically depict human heads. The naturalistic Mississippian head vases fall within a stylistic continuum that encompasses highly stylized depictions. Because the eyes are frequently closed, it has been suggested that head vases were connected with mortuary rituals or were ceramic representations of trophy heads.[44]

Griffin pointed out that head vases came predominantly from sites along the Mississippi River, rather than from those along the St. Francis River, and suggested that head vases found in the latter area were imported. The distinctive interior-beveled lip on the orifice of the Fortune head vase is a feature typically found in the former area, apparently dating to A.D. 1450−1600.[45]

In his February 2, 1880, letter to Putnam, written from Fortune Mounds, Curtiss stated that while he was at that site he had "bought 53 fine pieces." Among those, he continued, "One of the pieces are in shape like a fish or what is called a buffalo fish"— the genus *Ictiobus*. This is an evident reference to the finely modeled buffalo fish effigy bowl (pl. 14 and cover) catalogued as being from a "grave 3 feet deep" at Fortune.

The abundance of fish bones in prehistoric middens in the Mississippi alluvial valley demonstrates that fish, like other aquatic animals, were important to the Mississippians' livelihood. Yet we can only speculate why Indian potters depicted the buffalo fish to the exclusion of other economically important species. For that matter, the repertoire of animals depicted on Mississippian effigies offers a highly selective picture of the fauna that shared the floodplain with the early Indians. The anthropologist Claude Lévi-Strauss reminds us, however, that species may be chosen to appear in myths not because they are good to eat but because they are good to think with.[46] Southeastern Indian ethnography records that animals and birds had metaphorical connotations derived from their character in specific traditional narratives. In a Cherokee story, for instance, the tufted titmouse and the Carolina chickadee are paired as a liar and a truth teller, respectively, because of the deceptive similarity of their songs; the short tongue of the titmouse memorializes its punishment for lying.[47] One suspects that each of the kinds of creatures depicted in pottery effigies had such a cultural meaning, which was plain and obvious to the ancient potters and their community but is lost to us today.

Of course, buffalo fish can be very good eating, too.

IN HIS ST. FRANCIS RIVER writings, Edwin Curtiss consistently referred to the early inhabitants of the ancient village sites where he was working as "the old race." A close reading of these documents shows that Curtiss very likely believed that the "mound builders" were a people who had preceded and were distinct from Indians of the historic era. In an undated narrative recounting his explorations at Fortune Mounds and other sites, Curtiss wrote,

> I find intrusions[.] I mean by that there is people who buried there dead diferant‐ ly from the ones who built the Mounds or who lay at the bottom of the mounds which is reasonable to supose built the mounds and inhabited them long before the Indians for I find no pottery with them[.] some evidence of copper ornaments are ocassionaly found with the intruders but this evidence is nearly obliterated[.] only the stain and scales of oxide of copper remains to tell that it was once copper and allso in many instances I find them buried setting while the others the original ones are in evry instance put away in a horizontal position and more or less pieces of pottery found with them showing that they were remembered by there friends or relations after death and in all cases I find them under the intruders[.][48]

The "myth of the mound builders" was popular in the nineteenth century, but it is curious that Curtiss subscribed to it. For his employer and mentor, Frederic Ward Putnam, it was unproblematical that the people in the graves Curtiss had excavated along the St. Francis River were Indians. Putnam wrote in 1881, "That these remains from Arkansas are those of a people who were the immediate ancestors of the village Indians of that region, mentioned by the early writers, is very probable."[49]

During the time Curtiss was at Neeley's Ferry, he sent one of his assistants to exca‐ vate at Halcomb Mounds, which we know today as Togo. This work resulted in a col‐ lection of more than two hundred pottery vessels and other objects that are now among the Curtiss materials at the Peabody. Curtiss's correspondence with Putnam includes few descriptive details pertaining to Halcomb Mounds and few details about the contexts of the objects excavated there. His sketch map of the Neeley's Ferry site environs (see p. 23), however, portrays Halcomb Mounds as consisting of eight mounds enclosed by a "water ditch." Neither the ditch nor the mounds were observable at the Togo site in the late twentieth century.

Among the fifteen effigies collected by Curtiss's associates at Halcomb Mounds is a well-preserved cat-serpent bowl (pl. 21). In the 1951 *Survey* volume, James B. Griffin concluded that the classic "serpent-cat" effigy form was most characteristic of the Walls–Pecan Point area along the Mississippi River, with only "a number of crude representations" in the St. Francis area. Modern students of Mississippian iconography have seen the cat-serpent effigies, with their attributes of a feline face with open mouth and bared teeth, the eye markings of a falcon, and a snaky tail, as representations of the cosmological Underworld Monster, or Piasa. In this argument, cat-serpent effigy vessels are part of an iconography and style system encompassing depictions in diverse media, including stone and ceramic pipes, repoussé copper, and shell gorgets.[50]

Whereas Griffin characterized typical St. Francis–region cat-serpents, such as the Halcomb example, as "crude representations," it might be better to view them as cursive or hieratic treatments of the theme. In particular, the "toothy mouth" motif (see pl. 21, detail) is recognizable across the full range of media involved, including mud glyphs found deep in Southeastern caves.[51] More elaborately worked cat-serpent effigies from regions along the Mississippi River demonstrate the rationale for viewing cat-serpent vessels as part of a pan-Southeastern iconographic tradition.

We have meager evidence for the ways in which prehistoric Indians used effigy vessels. Fragments of effigies are extremely infrequent in midden deposits on Mississippian village sites. This suggests that most of the effigy vessels ever made were ultimately buried in graves. Notwithstanding, occasional cooking residues on effigy vessels and the more frequent presence of abrasion on their bases suggests that before they were buried in graves, these vessels saw use in warming or serving food. One imagines a scene similar to that recounted by Henri Joutel for the Quapaws in the village of Touriman at the mouth of the Arkansas River in 1687:

We took notice of some peculiar ceremonies, which we had not seen among the other nations. One of them is, that they serve up their meat in two or four large

Cat-serpent vessel from the Beck site, Crittenden County, Arkansas. Courtesy University of Arkansas Museum, catalogue number 30-2-486; photograph by Jane Kellett.

dishes, which are first set down before the two principal guests, who are at one end, and when they have eaten a little, those dishes are shov'd down lower and others are served in their place, in the same manner; so that the first dishes are served at the upper end and thrust down lower as others come in.[52]

Among the Curtiss materials at the Peabody Museum are fifty specimens, including pottery vessels, a pipe, bone implements, and a celt, that are catalogued as being from "Robinson Mounds." Judging from Curtiss's sketch map of Fortune Mounds and vicinity, it seems that Robinson Mounds corresponds to the site we know today as Turnbow. Robert Mainfort and Sarah Demb, however, have pointed out inconsistencies that suggest that this provenance may be erroneous.[53] On the Fortune Mounds environs map, Curtiss's annotation beside Robinson Mounds reads, "did no work here." Moreover, the location given for the "Robinson Mounds" specimens in the Peabody catalogue corresponds instead to that of a site in the immediate vicinity of

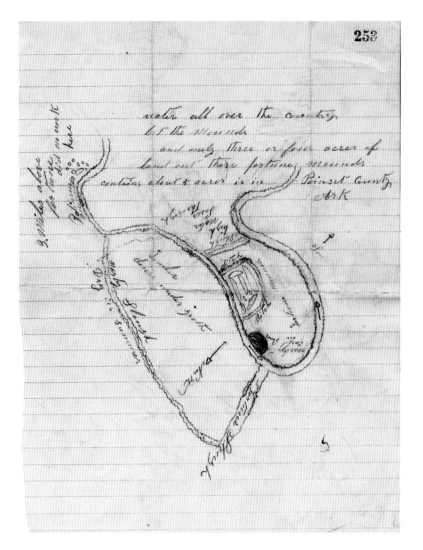

Curtiss's sketch map of Fortune Mounds and environs. North is toward bottom left. Accession file 80-20, Peabody Museum Archives, Harvard University.

Neeley's Ferry that Curtiss called "Love Mounds." From Curtiss's map of the environs of the Neeley's Ferry site (see p. 23), it is evident that "Love Mounds" is the site known today as Williamson. The "Robinson Mounds" specimens, wherever they came from, include only two fragmentary effigy vessels.

"I Am Afraid that I Shall Be Interfeared with by High Water"

Curtiss appears to have left Fortune Mounds around the end of February 1880. On March 3 he wrote to Putnam from Memphis, mentioning an enclosed "bill of loding" for eleven boxes of specimens weighing together twelve hundred pounds, which he referred to elsewhere in the letter as "250 pieces of pottery and ten or more cranias with a large or fine lot of stones, flints, curious and discard[ed] bones." These were evidently the fruits of his work at Fortune Mounds, Halcomb Mounds, and possibly other sites. Curtiss went on: "I am afraid that I shall be interfeared with [by] high water[.] the earth is cover[e]d with water all around me whare I am exploring but will hardly get over the mounds whare I am exploring for then it will be cover[e]d with stock[.] there is five acres in the mound field [Curtiss may have been referring to Fortune Mounds] and there will be hardly standing room for the stock."

Curtiss wrote Putnam again two days later. "I will go back to Ark this evening or start for camp and if the water does not interfere with explorations I will give you a good many pieces and get out of Ark by the first of April[.] my hands are sick and tired

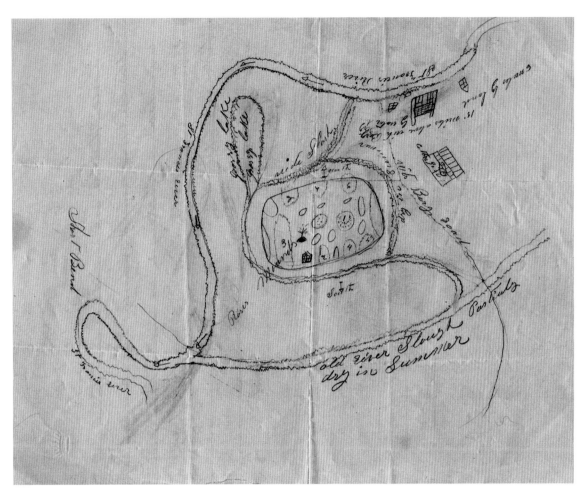

Curtiss's sketch map of Rose Mound. North is at left. Accession file 80-20, Peabody Museum Archives, Harvard University.

and played out[.] money don't appease there murmers[.] the wet we[a]ther, mosquitoes, buffalo knats and added to home sickness makes it a disagre[e]able camp[.]"

Two weeks of fieldwork at Rose Mound followed. By March 17, Curtiss was back in
Memphis, writing, "My Dear Mr. Putnam: I this day ship you three more large boxes
of relics by rail; today by merchants dispatch[.] the last you will receive from me til

Panorama of Rose Mound in 1947, from the southwest. Peabody Museum, LMS Archives, Box 71, neg. 47/1-10,11. Originally published as figure 74c in Phillips, Ford, and Griffin, *Archaeological Survey of the Lower Mississippi Alluvial Valley, 1940–1947* (1951).

this overflow subsides[.] a person who has never been here cant conceive how ter[r]ible it is in times like this here[.] if you want to stir out of the house there is the gum tree canoes or dugout[.] the mounds are out of water but a constant fall of rain and the earth is full of water[.]"

Curtiss recounted his fieldwork at Rose Mound in an undated narrative mailed to Putnam from Nashville on March 24, 1880.

> I left Fortune on ac[coun]t of poor luck, hard work and poor finds[.] I went down the St. Francis River to Mr. W. B. Roses 50 miles below Fortune an[d] explored in his mound field 1/4 of a mile from the St [Francis] River and here I found a mound that contained 15-1/2 acres that is a place that is surrounded by water spring & fall and winter[.] this field is 15 feet higher than the surrounding country and the field is covered by smaller mounds or ridges and they are full of human remains, burnt brick–like material, ashes, chard wood, fragments of pottery, flints fragments celts, petrified wood, hickory principally, and fragments of discoidal stones[.]

Curtiss went on to write that in the mounds he had found "pottery with animal shaped handles, some in the shape of fish, owls & other birds[.]"

Curtiss's sketch map of "Roses Mounds" (p. 37) shows some twenty mounds of varying sizes on the surface of the large, artificial elevation, as well as one contemporary house. Several buildings, including a cotton gin, are shown to the northeast of the site adjacent to "Wits Berg road."

From the day I first picked up a copy of the 1951 *Survey* volume during my high-school years in the 1960s, my favorite image in the book was the composite panorama of Rose Mound. The aspect of no other site so strongly evokes the magnitude of the St. Francis region's late prehistoric Indian presence. I first visited Rose Mound on a gray, rainy morning in August 1966. Ragged clouds scudded above the western horizon where Crowley's Ridge stretched along the skyline. Though the mounds that Curtiss observed on the surface of the vast village midden at Rose had long since disappeared, I found the place otherwise much as Curtiss had, with the damp ground under the cotton rows thickly littered with potsherds, fragments of burned clay daub, chipped stone debris, and animal bones.

At Rose Mound, Curtiss and his co-workers collected about 450 catalogued specimens, including pottery vessels and pipes, stone arrow points and celts, marine shell objects including beads and a mask, animal bones, and a fragment of a charred basket. These specimens include at least ten whole or fragmentary effigy vessels.

The Lower Mississippi Archaeological Survey went into abeyance with the outbreak of World War II at the end of 1941. Following the war, Rose Mound was one of the sites to which Philip Phillips returned to conduct stratigraphic excavations, accompanied by Ruth Phillips and Harvard graduate student Paul Gebhard. Phillips chose Rose Mound for stratigraphic study because it was the only large St. Francis–type site he and his colleagues had visited that showed significant quantities of pre-Mississippian clay-tempered pottery. The excavation at Rose was conducted in April 1947 with the help of a crew of local workmen. They dug through more than two and one-half meters of artifact-bearing deposits. On their way down, they encountered first the typical thick, frequently decorated, shell-tempered pottery of what has come to be called the Parkin phase, and then a stratum with thin, predominantly plain shell-tempered Mississippian pottery. At the bottom of the excavation, with the walls of the pit towering over the head of the shovel-wielding local crewman, they hit a stratum with grog-tempered pottery that we now attribute to the Baytown period, dating between A.D. 400 and 700. [54]

From the time of the Phillips, Ford, and Griffin survey, archaeologists have tried to understand the antecedents of the vibrant Indian society that built fortified villages along the banks of the St. Francis River and buried its dead with pottery vessels that included finely made painted and effigy forms. Phyllis and Dan Morse of the Arkansas Archeological Survey conducted an intensive survey in the immediate vicinity of the Parkin site in the late 1970s, identifying many previously unrecorded small archaeological sites. [55] On alluvial ridges along the old Mississippi River channel scar now occupied by the Tyronza River, they found sites with the large stone dart points and fire-cracked chert and quartzite that are the hallmarks of Archaic occupation, dating as early as 3000 B.C. Grog-tempered Baytown pottery dating to the Woodland period, between 500 B.C. and A.D. 700, was found in twenty-three locations in the survey area.

The Morses were particularly intrigued by the thirteen small Mississippian sites in the immediate vicinity of the Parkin site. These included sites with plain shell-tempered pottery, notched arrow points, [56] and fragments of polished chert hoes. To the Morses, these characteristics suggested Mississippian culture occupation in the A.D. 1000–1350 interval, predating the Parkin phase. Subsequently, the Morses advanced the bold hypothesis that, prior to 1350, Indians in the St. Francis region—and indeed much of this portion of the Mississippi Valley—lived in communities of scattered farmsteads. After that date, the Morses proposed, dramatic population movements and prevalent warfare forced people to move into large communities defended by ditches and palisades. It was in these large, compact, fortified towns, the Morses argued, that the ritual and artistic florescence took place that we see manifested in the elaborate painted and effigy pottery of the final centuries of the precontact era. [57]

The Morses' historical scenario remains to be verified by detailed and closely dated studies of many archaeological sites across the full range of sizes and configurations. In the summer of 1999, a team of archaeologists and volunteers led by Jeffrey M. Mitchem identified vestiges of a Mississippian community of dispersed houses, like that proposed by the Morses for the 1000–1350 interval, at a site located beside

Interstate 40 near the Parkin exit. The Meador site was then being leveled by heavy machinery to improve the field for rice cultivation. Radiocarbon dates from Meador indicated that the Mississippian occupation occurred in the 1200s or 1300s. Graves were associated with some of the Mississippian house foundations at Meador. Following the salvage excavation, the landowner, the archaeologists, and representatives of the Quapaw Tribe cooperated in reburying the human remains from the Meador site at a nearby location that will be preserved as a cemetery.[58]

Study of human skeletal remains excavated over many decades is deepening our understanding of both life and death among the people who lived in the late prehistoric villages of the St. Francis River country. This research has been spurred most recently by the need for compliance with the Native American Graves Protection and Repatriation Act.[59] Archaeologists have collaborated with biological anthropologists to analyze more than five hundred human remains from six sites in the Parkin phase, including Neeley's Ferry, Vernon Paul, and Parkin.[60]

High rates of dental caries (tooth decay), combined with skeletal symptoms of iron deficiency anemia, indicate that the late prehistoric Indians of the St. Francis River consumed substantial amounts of maize but comparatively little red meat. The Parkin phase people, in common with their contemporaries in adjacent regions, also show high rates of osteophytosis (spinal arthritis) and high incidences of nonspecific skeletal responses to infection. Osteophytosis can reflect stress from chronic strenuous physical activity. High incidences of infections may be related to inadequate nutrition and social stress as well as exposure to disease germs.

Researchers have remarked that the people of the Parkin phase and its neighbors stand out in precontact North America for their comparatively high rates of skeletal indicators of infection and unbalanced nutrition. These may have been consequences of year-round residence in crowded, unsanitary, fortified villages and an overdependence on maize. Despite these conditions, it is clear that at some junctures in their history, the late prehistoric Indians of the St. Francis River thrived and became a numerous people.

CURTISS WROTE Putnam again a few days after his arrival in Nashville, declaring his intention to resume collecting for the museum as soon as possible, this time in middle Tennessee. In this letter Curtiss stated that he was sending Putnam, by the same mail, his bill of expenses and "allso field notes, plats or rough pencil sketches of various mounds."

Putnam and Curtiss continued to correspond over the ensuing weeks, sorting out the expenses of the Arkansas expedition. Curtiss furnished a detailed accounting of the field gear that had been entrusted to him. He also shared news about further archaeological collecting in Tennessee, about his wife's serious illness and partial recovery, and about his resuming, for the time being, his career in public works by taking on the construction of a large sewer in Nashville. Curtiss asked Putnam's advice about the prospect of his joining expeditions to Mexico and Central America. He had earlier expressed an intention to accept Putnam's invitation to visit Cambridge, "which is one of the great desires of my life which I hope to see once before I join the old race our friends the Mound Builders."

Curtiss never visited Cambridge or returned to Arkansas. On December 6, 1880, he died suddenly of a heart attack in Nashville at the age of fifty.

Putnam eulogized Curtiss in a footnote in his 1881 annual report for the museum. After recounting the essential facts about Curtiss's life, death, and career, Putnam went on to write,

> Mr. Curtis had a sturdy honest character, which combined with the large practical experience he had obtained and a knowledge of handling his men, rendered him unusually well qualified for the hard and rough labor he undertook for the Museum, while his enthusiastic zeal in its behalf was not only a great source of pleasure to me, but resulted in making many strong friends for the Museum in the South, to whom we are under many obligations.[61]

Elsewhere in the report, Putnam discussed the remarkable collection of several thousand specimens obtained by Curtiss and summarized Curtiss's field observations. "The whole collection," Putnam wrote, "has been within the past month arranged in the Moundbuilders' room, and it will ever be a memorial of a most faithful and devoted friend of the Museum."[62]

Now, more than a century later, Edwin Curtiss's legacy continues to enrich North

American archaeology and Indian history. Researchers find that Mississippian pottery effigies reward painstaking study of individual pieces and systematic analysis of their seemingly endless variety. Among the Curtiss effigies, certain vessels are almost identical to other vessels in the Peabody's collection or in collections at other museums, but one is nonetheless struck by the formal variety among the series as a whole. When confronted with broad stylistic diversity within a limited geographical area, archaeologists often suspect that they are looking at objects produced over a substantial span of time. Indeed, it is likely that the effigy pottery from the St. Francis region represents several generations of potters and sequences of stylistic development. The frog bowl, the wood duck rim-effigy bowl, and the cat-serpent bowl reflect widespread Mississippian subjects and themes. Ancient potters in the St. Francis River region, however, offered distinctive treatments of some of these themes (see, for example, the wood duck effigies in pls. 5 and 8 and the cat-serpent in pl. 21). These St. Francis–region styles contrast in many cases with those of regions bordering the Mississippi River.

In Mississippian effigies, one catches faint echoes not only of Native American myth (e.g., the cat-serpent, pl. 21) but also of the visual language employed by ceramic artists of several centuries ago. Silhouette outlines of the heads of birds appear to have been cut from thick, flat sheets of clay and finished retaining the rectangular cross-section (pls. 3, 5, 8). Wings of birds are portrayed either by appliquéd fillets (pl. 13) or by painting, with primary feathers rendered as parallel lines (pl. 22). Future scholars may construct grammars of the visual style systems of Mississippian effigies.[63]

Formal characteristics of individual vessels, such as the head vase that Curtiss's "hands" excavated at Fortune Mounds (pl. 15), hint that they were imported to the St. Francis River country from other regions. Chemical composition studies may help distinguish imported vessels from locally produced ones.[64] Future scholars studying Mississippian ceramic effigies alongside Mississippian art in other media will formulate hypotheses about changing patterns of isolation and interaction among regional artistic traditions in prehistory. Archaeologists suspect that ceramic styles diffused and that elaborate painted, engraved, and effigy vessels and other artworks were exchanged in the context of shifting alliances formed among Native tribes, confederations, and chiefdoms.

The populous and vibrant Indian societies that existed along the St. Francis River, as well as their contemporaries up and down the Mississippi Valley, disappeared in the decades following the Spanish explorations in the mid-sixteenth century.[65] Scholars debate the causes. Pandemics of Old World diseases such as smallpox, measles, and malaria may have contributed to a demographic collapse.[66] Climate scholars have recently identified evidence for a severe and prolonged continental-scale drought that occurred during this critical historical juncture.[67] Waves of political instability emanating from nascent European colonization on the Gulf and Atlantic coasts may also have played a role.[68] It is unlikely, however, that the people themselves disappeared without a trace; presumably there were survivors who dispersed to become parts of other political formations. Their descendents may appear in colonial history in other places under names such as Quapaw, Koroa, and Tunica.

Whatever the immediate causes, one era had ended and another had begun. The Native towns of closely spaced houses surrounded by palisades were abandoned and fell into ruin, becoming, together with their adjacent fields, covered by forest. Except for transient Indian and French hunters who left few physical traces of their sojourns, the sites remained uninhabited for nearly two centuries, until the influx of American settlement in the decades following the War of 1812.

Edwin Curtiss's letters and narratives convey the excitement and wonder he experienced during his pioneering investigations on the banks of the St. Francis River. Generations of archaeologists since, from Clarence B. Moore, Philip Phillips, James A. Ford, and James B. Griffin to Charles R. McGimsey, Hester Davis, Dan and Phyllis Morse, and Jeffrey M. Mitchem—and many others—have felt the same awe and inspiration, as well as deep scientific curiosity. The remarkable pottery collections from the region, such as the Peabody Museum's Curtiss collection and the hundreds of vessels from the University of Arkansas Museum's 1930s excavations, have similarly inspired wonder in generations of researchers. The images in clay that have resided for over a century in the Peabody Museum promise not only new insights from scientific study but also glimpses of Indian artists' visions from a vanished world in Arkansas's Mississippi River lowlands in the last centuries of prehistory.

Color Plates

PLATE 1
Frog effigy jar
79-4-10/20176.1
Stanly Mounds (Parkin),
Mississippian culture, A.D. 1200–1600
Shell-tempered earthenware
Length 14.0 cm, height 8.0 cm,
mouth diameter 12.8 cm

AFTER FISH, frogs are the most frequent subjects for whole vessel effigies at late prehistoric sites in the St. Francis River region. The shape of this small effigy approximates the standard Mississippian-culture jar form. To this basic shape, the potter added small head and tail features and four smoothed–down fillets to represent the limbs. On the head, the eyes are rendered in low relief by small, flattened nodes. No mouth is represented, and no attempt was made to represent the digits on the ends of the limbs. Regularly spaced nicks encircling the lip are a common feature of utilitarian jars and bowls. The paired suspension holes on either side of the rim suggest that the vessel was hung by a rope or cord, perhaps over a fire to warm its contents. Curtiss's notes state that this vessel came from a grave in Mound 1. (T4585. Hillel S. Burger, photographer.)

PLATE 2
Red and white painted conch shell effigy
79-4-10/20191
Stanly Mounds (Parkin),
Mississippian culture, A.D. 1200–1600
Shell-tempered earthenware with
red pigmented and white
pigmented slips
Length 25.8 cm (including
restored spout), width 20.8 cm,
height 10.0 cm

THIS VESSEL was modeled after cups fashioned from the shells of large whelks. The exterior bears bold designs in red and white. The white (or cream-colored) slip appears to have been applied to the negative spaces of the red design with care not to overlap or smear the red. The spire (or top) and side of the shell form are separate fields of design. The design on the spire includes two bold red circles and two bold semicircular lines between the apex and the knobbed juncture of the spire and the first whorl. The remainder of the vessel, corresponding to the first whorl of a shell, displays a red herringbone pattern composed of three parallel zigzag lines running the length of the base and dovetailing with V-shaped elements pendant from the rim. The entire interior is red. The hollow knob corresponding to the apex of the spire may have functioned as a finger- or thumb-hold for the vessel; much of the paint on the adjacent vessel exterior is worn away, perhaps from use. Historical documents from the Southeast portray Indians drinking the ceremonial, caffeine-laced "Black Drink" from conch shell vessels. Black Drink was brewed from the parched leaves of *yaupon,* a native holly. This vessel exhibits minor restoration by museum conservators in the spout area and interior. Curtiss's notes record that the vessel came from Mound 3. (Opposite: T4578; at left: T4588. Hillel S. Burger, photographer.)

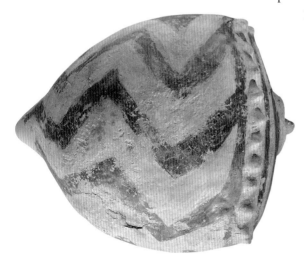

49

PLATE 3
Bird rim effigy bowl
80-20-10/21053
Neeley's Ferry Mounds, Mississippian
culture, A.D. 1200–1600
Shell-tempered earthenware
Length 21.9 cm, width 16.6 cm,
height 16.7 cm

BIRDS ARE the most common subjects of rim effigies along the St. Francis River. The broken rim effigy on this hemispherical bowl was mended by museum conservators. The flat, silhouette-like configuration of the head and squarish cross section of the beak suggest that the maker cut the appended piece from a slab of clay. The edge of the distinctive crest, however, was rounded into a semi-circle. The bird's eyes are bold raised circles; the eye on the right takes a flattened, truncated conical form. The potter formed the tail as an unelaborated half-moon tab. The base of the vessel is heavily abraded, perhaps from use. (T4404.1. Hillel S. Burger, photographer.)

PLATE 4
Bird rim effigy jar
80-20-10/21076
Neeley's Ferry Mounds, Mississippian
culture, A.D. 1200–1600
Shell-tempered earthenware
Length 26.7 cm (incomplete),
width 22.9 cm, height 20.3 cm

THIS UNUSUALLY LARGE effigy is also unusual in that the vessel form corresponds to that of the prevalent cooking jar of the Parkin phase—deep in profile, with a rounded base and slightly constricted rim. The beak and a portion of the rim are missing. Bulges in the contour at the front and back of the neck at rim level suggest that the potter added clay inside and out to buttress the effigy head attachment. The profile of the remaining portion of the head and the bold rendering of the eyes, which are thick, rounded disks with pupils formed by punctations, suggest that the subject is a wood duck (*Aix sponsa*). On the rim opposite the head, a broad, unelaborated, half-moon tab represents the tail. Vestiges of black, carbonaceous material on the rim exterior may be soot or cooking residue. (T4415.1. Hillel S. Burger, photographer.)

PLATE 5
Bird rim effigy bowl
80-20-10/21110.1
Neeley's Ferry Mounds, Mississippian
culture, A.D. 1200–1600
Shell-tempered earthenware
Length 23.6 cm, width 19.8 cm,
height 13.6 cm

INWARD-FACING HEADS on rim effigies suggest that one is looking at stylized ventral (belly-upward) portrayals of the subjects. The head on this vessel has a squarish cross section, hinting that it was modeled by cutting the outline from a thick slab of clay. The eyes appear to have been formed by adding clay, smoothing it down, and then accentuating the features with excision. Sparse vestiges of dark carbonaceous material, which may be soot or charred food residue, are present on the rim exterior. On the rim opposite the head, a prominent, unelaborated half-moon tab corresponds to the tail. The base is abraded. (T4588.2. Hillel S. Burger, photographer.)

PLATE 6
Fish effigy bowl
80-20-10/21118
Neeley's Ferry Mounds, Mississippian
culture, A.D. 1200–1600
Shell-tempered earthenware
Length 15.2 cm (incomplete),
width 14.6 cm, height 6.4 cm

SEEN HERE from above, this hemispherical bowl represents the stylized profile of a buffalo fish. The features of the fish are appliquéd to the circular rim of the vessel. On the sturdy head appendage, which may have served as a handle, smoothed-down nodes on either surface of the head render eyes. A fillet of clay, thinned toward the edge, indicates the dorsal fin, with fine wet-paste incision rendering the bony rays. The similar "ventral fin" is a stylization, not corresponding to the anatomy of a buffalo fish. The tail appendage (with the end broken off) is also quite sturdy, similarly suggesting use as a handle. Fish, typically buffalo fish, are the most common subjects of Mississippian effigies along the St. Francis River. The downward-directed mouth on this effigy is a specific characteristic of the smallmouth buffalo fish (*Ictiobus bubalus*). (Opposite: T4418.1; below: T4405.1. Hillel S. Burger, photographer.)

PLATE 7
Bird rim effigy bowl
80-20-10/21125
Neeley's Ferry Mounds, Mississippian
culture, A.D. 1200–1600
Shell-tempered earthenware
Length 28.7 cm, width 19.9 cm,
height 15.3 cm

THIS EFFIGY had been broken, but when museum conservators pre-pared it to be photographed for this book, they found sufficient fragments to reconstruct most of the vessel. The bird's head is shown with a longitu-dinal crest extending from the middle of the top of the head backward. As finished, the effigy lacks any representation of the eyes of the bird, though a faint bump on the left side of the head may be the vestige of an eye that was erased. The mouth is rendered by a jagged, dry incision in an elongated oval wrapping around the front of the beak. The large crest at the back of the head and the rendering of the mouth in the long beak suggest a large, possibly a pileated, woodpecker "whooping"—making its loud, ringing call—with its beak open and tongue displayed. The base of the vessel shows heavy abrasion that may be from use. (T4385.1. Hillel S. Burger, photographer.)

PLATE 8
Bird rim effigy bowl
80-20-10/21131
Neeley's Ferry Mounds, Mississippian
culture, A.D. 1200–1600
Shell-tempered earthenware
Length 21.9 cm, width 16.6 cm,
height 13.2 cm

THIS RIM EFFIGY, with its inward-facing head, is similar to 80-20-10/21110.1 (pl. 5), also from Neeley's Ferry. The excising around the eyes, however, is more prominent, and the beak is more pointed. Certain "field marks"—a broad crest, strong eye pattern, short beak, and short neck— suggest that the effigy represents a wood duck, a year-round resident of southern swamp forests. The tail is a plain, slightly downturned hemispherical tab. A carbonaceous encrustation on the rim exterior may be cooked food residue. Spalling of the exterior also suggests use of the vessel for cooking. Bird effigy heads with squarish edges, seemingly formed by cutting the silhouette from a thick slab of clay, appear to be a St. Francis regional style. (T4416.1. Hillel S. Burger, photographer.)

PLATE 9
Bird rim effigy bowl
80-20-10/21147
Neeley's Ferry Mounds, Mississippian
culture, A.D. 1200–1600
Shell-tempered earthenware,
polished
Length 23.2 cm, width 16.0 cm,
height 12.8 cm

PHILLIPS, FORD, AND GRIFFIN illustrated this rim effigy bowl, with its elaborately fenestrated head and tail appendages, in their 1951 *Survey* volume. The breakage pattern on the head suggests that the neck and face and the beak and hood (or crest) were modeled as two separate elements and then assembled on the horizontal flange attached to the rim. The fenestrated tail, similarly, appears to have been modeled separately and attached to the vessel rim as a single element. The flange under the head may have functioned as a handle. This vessel was broken and glued back together with minor restoration of the face area. Curtiss recorded in his field notes that this was one of six vessels from a child's grave. (T4420.1. Hillel S. Burger, photographer.)

PLATE 10
Bird rim effigy bowl
80-20-10/21190
Neeley's Ferry Mounds, Mississippian
culture, A.D. 1200–1600
Shell-tempered earthenware
Maximum length 22.5 cm,
height 14.8 cm

THIS EFFIGY on a hemispherical bowl portrays an unidentified species of bird with a prominent crest, large eyes, and a broad, thick bill with a rounded tip and a conspicuous longitudinal ridge on its upper side. The head is modeled in the round, leaving few clues to construction techniques. The eyes, rendered as large flattened cones, recall those on 80-20-10/21053 (pl. 3). The conspicuously broad tab tail probably refers to a particular species. The base exhibits abrasion. (T4384.1. Hillel S. Burger, photographer.)

65

PLATE 11
Opossum effigy bowl
80-20-10/21226
Neeley's Ferry Mounds, Mississippian
culture, A.D. 1200–1600
Shell-tempered earthenware
Length 18.7 cm, height 12.0 cm

THIS EFFIGY BOWL embodies many of the conventions of frog bowls: the upturned snout pushed out from the interior, the flexed limbs rendered in relief by welded–down appliquéd strips, and digits rendered by cursive incision. The rounded ears with the pointed tips and the conspicuous nostrils formed by sharp punctations in the end of the pointed snout, however, indicate that the subject is an opossum. On the rear of the vessel, a triangular appliquéd element extending upward from the junction of the back legs appears to be a stylized representation of the animal's tail (see below). Museum curators mended cracks in the base of the vessel. Abrasion on the base may be from use. (Opposite: T4401.1; below: T4591.2. Hillel S. Burger, photographer.)

PLATE 12
Opossum effigy hooded bottle
80-20-10/21436
Fortune Mounds, Mississippian culture,
A.D. 1200–1600
Fine shell- and grog-tempered
earthenware
Diameter 8.7 cm, height 11.2 cm

HOODED EFFIGY BOTTLES (sometimes called gourd effigies) are a geographically widespread Mississippian form characterized by an orifice at the side of the upper portion of the vessel. The orifice is most commonly at the back of the head, as in this small, delicately modeled, zoomorphic example. The eyes on the front of the face, the pointed, upturned snout, and the small ears identify the effigy as an opossum. In addition to opossums, owls and humans were frequent subjects of hooded effigy bottles. (Opposite: T4595; below: T4581. Hillel S. Burger, photographer.)

PLATE 13

Bird rim effigy bowl
80-20-10/21455
Fortune Mounds, Mississippian culture,
A.D. 1200–1600
Shell-tempered earthenware
Length 22.5 cm, height 14.7 cm

POTTERS ALONG both the St. Francis River and the Mississippi rendered bird wings in relief by appliquéing strips of clay onto a bowl's exterior. On this vessel, the wing axis is placed above the pendant "feathers," rendering a "ventral" (from below) view of the wing. The domelike top of the head, the hooked beak, and the wattle on the front of the neck below the rim suggest a gallinaceous species such as a prairie chicken or turkey, or, alternatively, a turkey vulture. The tail is a short, broad tab attached at the lip and tilted downward. It ends in three points—perhaps intended to represent feathers—formed by cutting out the interstices between the points and subsequently smoothing them over (below). This vessel has been broken and glued back together. The right portion of the face is missing, and some restoration is evident on the right wing. The base exhibits abrasion that may be from use. (Opposite: T4417.2; below: T4590. Hillel S. Burger, photographer.)

PLATE 14
Fish effigy bowl
80-20-10/21459
Fortune Mounds, Mississippian culture,
A.D. 1200–1600
Shell- and grog-tempered
earthenware
Length 29.9 cm, height 8.0 cm

HERE A PREHISTORIC potter made exceptionally good use of the advantages of fine-grog-and-shell-tempered paste as a sculptural medium. The small mouth with protruding lips, prominent gill slits, and bifurcated tail indicate that the subject of this effigy is the bigmouth buffalo fish (*Ictiobus cyprinellus*). The mouth of this species is on the front of the head rather than downward-directed as on the smallmouth buffalo fish. The head, tail, and fin appendages appear to have been modeled separately and applied to the bowl's rim. The gill slits and rays on the fins, however, were incised in fairly dry paste, probably after the appendages had been attached. Each of the five appendages is set off from the vessel rim by a line of regular punctations executed in wet paste after the appendage was attached. Between each appendage, the rim is decorated with a line of evenly spaced appliquéd nodes. This effigy bowl had been repaired in the museum with some restoration in the bottom of the bowl. (Opposite: T4383.1; below: T4425.1. Hillel S. Burger, photographer.)

73

PLATE 15
Red and buff head vase
80-20-10/21542
Fortune Mounds, Mississippian culture,
A.D. 1200–1600
Shell- and grog-tempered
earthenware
Length 17.5 cm, height 19.0 cm

THE PEABODY MUSEUM'S head vase from Fortune Mounds is one of the most naturalistic Mississippian head vases. Its human head is depicted without a neck, and the base of the vessel is a flat surface extending from the chin to the back of the head. This gives the facial plane a marked upward slant, as if it was intended to be viewed from an elevated angle. The small perforation through the shelf above the center of the forehead might have been for the attachment of objects corresponding to the forelock beads seen on figures in prehistoric Southeastern shell art (see illustration on p. 30). The raised, teardrop-shaped element extending from the top of the forehead to the middle of the back of the head, encompassing the flaring neck of the vessel, may represent a man's roached hair arrangement. The thick, dark red slip on the surface surrounding the "roach" perhaps represents red paint worn on shaved portions of the crown of the head. The remaining ear has seven perforations, probably for the attachment of perishable objects such as feathers.

Chipping on the lip of the vessel, the wearing away of paint on the "roach" at the base of the flaring neck, and slight abrasion on the base may all be from use. (Opposite: T4392.1; left: T4390.1; right: T4391.1. Hillel S. Burger, photographer.)

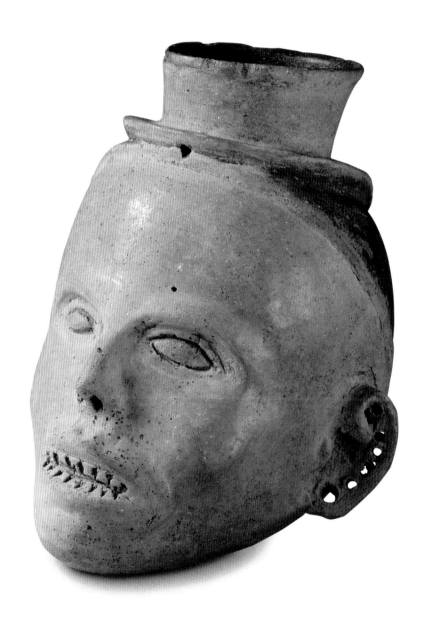

PLATE 16
Two-headed rim effigy jar
80-20-10/21753.1
Fortune Mounds, Mississippian culture,
A.D. 1200–1600
Shell-tempered earthenware
Length 20.1 cm, height 14.1 cm

THE PREHISTORIC Mississippian effigy vessel repertoire includes infrequent two-headed rim effigies. Here, on the zoomorphic, outward-facing head, the maker rendered the creature's eyes with globular appliquéd nodes. To form the mouth on the end of the muzzle, the potter pressed a stick or other slender cylindrical object horizontally into the clay. On the back of the inward-facing, anthropomorphic head is a deep circular impression, perhaps made by a thumb. The form of the vessel corresponds to that of a cooking jar. Abrasion is present on the base. A ring of whitish encrustation on the interior may be a calcareous precipitate leached from the sediments overlying the grave from which this vessel was excavated. (T4592. Hillel S. Burger, photographer.)

PLATE 17
Frog effigy jar
80-20-10/21545
Halcomb Mounds, Mississippian
culture, A.D. 1200–1600
Shell-tempered earthenware
Length 18.2 cm, height 8.3 cm

LIKE THE FROG EFFIGY from Stanly Mounds (pl. 1), this small effigy employs the basic shape of a jar, including the two rim lugs. Here, however, the potter constructed the forms of the head and tail by pushing out the vessel wall from the inside rather than by applying additional clay to the exterior. The eyes are rendered with shallow, well-smoothed-over depressions, and a bold, horizontal incised line indicates the mouth. Cursive incision, subsequently smoothed over, suggests the frog's fingers and toes. The black coating on the exterior of the body of the vessel may be soot or carbonized food residue. On the base, this black coating is abraded away. (T4593. Hillel S. Burger, photographer.)

PLATE 18
Miniature zoomorphic rim effigy bowl
80-20-10/21553
Halcomb Mounds, Mississippian
culture, A.D. 1200–1600
Shell-tempered earthenware
Length 12.9 cm (incomplete),
height 7.2 cm

THIS MINIATURE BOWL exhibits a variant treatment of the cat–serpent theme. The head and neck appear to have been formed by pinching the top of a subtriangular or prismatic bar of clay to create the concavities surrounding each eye and the pointed ears. Shallow punctations with a hollow, reedlike implement rendered the eyes. The bending forward of the head and neck and the prominent, pinched-out snout or muzzle—as well as the tail on the opposite side of the rim—contradict the owl-like aspect of the face and suggest that the subject is, after all, the cat–serpent being. Also varying from the usual treatment of the theme, the serpent tail is formed from a disk of clay; its circular fenestration appears to have been formed around a dowel-like object. Like the head, the tail is applied to the top of a thickened flange running along the rim. (T4413.1. Hillel S. Burger, photographer.)

PLATE 19
Fish effigy bottle
80-20-10/21572
Halcomb Mounds, Mississippian
culture, A.D. 1200–1600
Shell-tempered earthenware
Length 20.4 cm, height 19.5 cm

TREATMENTS OF THE buffalo–fish theme by Mississippian potters include bottles with depictions of the fish swimming in a natural position. On the face of this effigy, the eyes are rendered with flattened appliquéd nodes, and the mouth with a circular depression apparently chiseled out of almost dry clay. Posterior to the face, shallow, polished–over, finger–width grooves indicate gill slits. The dorsal and tail fins are subtly indicated by low, rounded flanges of clay. Four damaged appendages on the base of the vessel probably represent fins but also functioned as supports. Abrasion on the broken faces of the supports may be prehistoric use wear.

The rounded mouth at the end of the head, the large eyes, the conspicuous gill slits, and the hint of a bifurcated tail identify the subject of this effigy as the big–mouth buffalo fish. Tall, wide necks are frequent on Mississippian bottles in the St. Francis region. (Opposite: T4388.1; at left: T4389.1. Hillel S. Burger, photographer.)

PLATE 20
Hooded effigy bottle
80-20-10/21614
Halcomb Mounds, Mississippian
culture, A.D. 1200–1600
Shell-tempered earthenware
Length 11.5 cm, height 12.3 cm

INSIDE THIS VESSEL is a penciled note on a scrap of pink paper, evidently in Curtiss's hand, referring to it as a "hanging bird's nest." This is presumably an allusion to the hanging nest of the northern oriole. Philip Phillips humorously characterized this form as the "lemon squeezer," but researchers generally acknowledge that it is a version of the widespread pointed, or "dunce cap," human effigy in which all human attributes have been conventionalized out of existence. In addition to the typical converging, notched, vertical ridges, this vessel includes an unusual knob at its apex. The horizontal fillet encircling the vessel from one side of the circular orifice to the other may be a stylized pair of arms. The base of the vessel is slightly abraded. Curtiss also found a miniature hooded bottle at Halcomb Mounds (below). The holes in its apex may have been used to suspend the vessel. (Opposite: T4400.1; below: T4430.1. Hillel S. Burger, photographer.)

Miniature hooded bottle from
Halcomb Mounds, 80-20-10/21632, height 9 cm

PLATE 21
Cat-serpent rim effigy bowl
80-20-10/21621
Halcomb Mounds, Mississippian
culture, A.D. 1200–1600
Shell-tempered earthenware,
polished
Length 27.1 cm, width 21.0 cm,
height (incomplete) 16.1 cm

THE CAT-SERPENT, a mythological being with attributes of a carnivore, a serpent, and sometimes a falcon, is one of the most common Mississippian effigy-vessel themes in the central Mississippi Valley. This vessel represents a common St. Francis River style variant of the cat–serpent. The head and neck appear to have been formed from a single elongated block of clay and then smoothly welded onto the vessel body. The head was modeled by bending one end of the block forward and pinching out the snout and ears. No eyes are present. The oval mouth, incised by the prehistoric artisan when the clay was almost dry, is an example of the "toothy mouth" motif that appears to be associated with a cosmological Underworld Monster (below). The head is not a rattle like the heads of some cat–serpent effigies from the region bordering the Mississippi River. The curled tailed is modeled in the round with an upward–pointing tip element and a prominent fenestration. Curtiss unearthed an almost identical vessel from nearby Neeley's Ferry. (Opposite: T4411.1; below: T4412.1. Hillel S. Burger, photographer.)

PLATE 22
Red-on-buff bird effigy bottle
80-20-10/21639
Halcomb Mounds, Mississippian
culture, A.D. 1200–1600
Fine shell- and grog-tempered
earthenware with red mineral slip
Height 20.3 cm, length 19.7 cm

THIS STRIKING VESSEL from the Curtiss collection was illustrated by Clarence B. Moore in his 1910 report, "The Antiquities of the St. Francis, White and Black Rivers, Arkansas," and later by Phillips, Ford, and Griffin in their 1951 *Survey* volume. The effigy takes the form of the body of a bird with a broad, short tail—but minus the head. The base exhibits the remnants of four small feet or supports that have been broken off. Bold red stripes indicate wings, depicted in dorsal view as if folded against the body, with the vertical wing axis in front and horizontal primary feathers converging over the back. The painted lozenge-shaped elements seen on effigies such as this one—rendered either positively or negatively—were a convention for depicting the breast feather patterns of birds. The worn-off appearance of the paint on the neck is probably a result of people's handling it for months or years before the object was buried. Abrasion over the broken surfaces of the feet is probably also from prehistoric use. (Opposite: T4598.1; below: T4424.1. Hillel S. Burger, photographer.)

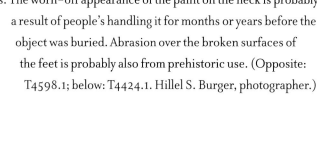

PLATE 23
Double-headed rim effigy bowl
80-20-10/21843
Rose Mound, Mississippian culture,
A.D. 1200–1600
Shell-tempered earthenware
Length 23.3 cm, width 20.6 cm,
height 15.9 cm

TWO ALMOST IDENTICAL effigy heads, both facing inward, are attached to opposite sides of the rim of this deep bowl. Each head exhibits a long muzzle, a bulge at the back of the head, and prominent ears formed by pyramidal bits of clay extending diagonally from the sides of the head. The eyes are rendered as bold punctations executed in wet paste with a cylindrical implement that may have been a hollow cane or reed. The base is smoothly abraded, perhaps from prehistoric use. The vessel was broken and mended, with a few pieces missing, and the surface has spalled away in places. Curtiss's field notes state that this vessel was one of seven found in a grave with "five bodies lying in a circle, hands to the center, pots in a pile." (T4409.1. Hillel S. Burger, photographer.)

PLATE 24
Bird rim effigy bowl
80-20-10/21995
Rose Mound, Mississippian culture,
A.D. 1200–1600
Shell-tempered earthenware
Length 28.7 cm, width 19.9 cm,
height 15.3 cm

THE DISTINCTIVE OUTLINE of the broad rim lug on this piece (on the portion of the rim opposite the head) probably represents the tail of a broad-tailed bird such as a vulture or turkey. Few clues for identification, however, are offered by the head, which is rendered in profile. The jutting lower neck below the rim may be a naturalistic feature such as a wattle, but it probably also served to buttress the juncture between the head and rim. Minor chipping and evident abrasion on the head suggest that it served as a handle. (T4397.1. Hillel S. Burger, photographer.)

PLATE 25
Red frog effigy bowl
80-20-10/22063
Rose Mound, Mississippian culture,
A.D. 1200–1600
Shell-tempered earthenware
and red mineral pigment
Length 14.5 cm, height 9.0 cm

AN ORANGE-RED SLIP with a very saturated color covers both the inside and outside of this small bowl with a restricted orifice. The exterior is highly polished, with myriad tiny, elongated facets from application of the polishing stone. The effigy features—head with eyes formed by flattened nodes, the fore and hind limbs, and the anal opening, rendered with a smoothed-down oval ring of clay—were applied to the exterior of the bowl prior to application of the red slip and subsequent polishing. The polish almost obscures the sharp incisions that render the digits on the ends of the limbs. Two pairs of holes just below the rim on either side of the vessel were apparently drilled through the vessel wall after firing. The base of the vessel exhibits a slight dulling of the polish, possibly from abrasion during use. (Opposite: T4597.1; below: T4414.1. Hillel S. Burger, photographer.)

NOTES

1. Kevin E. Smith, "Some Speculations on Curtiss, Thruston and Putnam," *Newsletter of the Middle Cumberland Archaeological Society* 28, no. 3 (2003): 2–4.

2. I have taken the particulars of Edwin Curtiss's five-month sojourn in Arkansas and the quotations from his correspondence with Putnam from Robert C. Mainfort Jr. and Sarah R. Demb, "Edwin Curtiss's Archaeological Explorations along the St. Francis River, Northeast Arkansas, 1879–1880," *Arkansas Archeologist* 41 (2001): 1–27. Mainfort and Demb also identify the archaeological sites investigated by Curtiss by their modern names and site numbers.

3. Philip Phillips, "Archaeological Survey in the Lower Yazoo Basin, Mississippi, 1949–1955," *Papers of the Peabody Museum of Archaeology and Ethnology* 60 (1970): 930–933.

4. The kind of archaeological collecting carried out by Curtiss and his contemporaries in the nineteenth century would be unacceptable today. NAGPRA, on the federal level, and recent state laws extending legal protection to unmarked graves of any age have begun to redress historic human rights disparities in this context. One of NAGPRA's results has been to bring Indians and archaeologists into unprecedented collaborations and to make them sometimes allies in promoting preservation of cultural resources. Since Curtiss's day, the prehistoric Indian villages and mounds of the region have been severely damaged by erosion, cultivation, and land leveling for farmland improvement, not to mention generations of relentless pothunters. For these reasons, the Curtiss collection, notwithstanding our reservations

today about the manner in which it was acquired, is a uniquely valuable resource for the study of Native American culture and history.

5. Clarence Bloomfield Moore, "Antiquities of the St. Francis, White and Black Rivers, Arkansas," *Journal of the Academy of Natural Science of Philadelphia,* 2d ser., 14 (1910): 255–364.

6. Jamie C. Brandon's recent master's thesis, "Death and the Parkin Phase: Mortuary Patterning in the Archeological Data Recovered from the Durham Excavations in North-eastern Arkansas, 1932–1933" (Department of Anthropology, University of Arkansas, Fayetteville, 1999), synthesizes results from the University of Arkansas Museum's early excavations in the Parkin area.

7. Philip Phillips, James A. Ford, and James B. Griffin, *Archaeological Survey in the Lower Mississippi Alluvial Valley, 1940–1947,* Papers of the Peabody Museum of American Archaeology and Ethnology 25 (1951). In 1946, Ford joined the staff of the American Museum of Natural History in New York City, which assumed cosponsorship of the Lower Mississippi Archaeological Survey in place of Louisiana State University.

8. Robert C. Dunnell, "Archaeological Survey in the Lower Mississippi Alluvial Valley, 1940–1947: A Landmark Study in American Archaeology," *American Antiquity* 50 (1985): 297–300.

9. Cyrus Thomas, *Report on the Mound Explorations of the Bureau of Ethnology,* Twelfth Annual Report of the Bureau of Ethnology (Washington, DC: Smithsonian Institution, 1894; reprint, Washington, DC: Smithsonian Institution Press, 1985).

10. W. H. Holmes, *Ancient Pottery of the Mississippi Valley,* Fourth Annual Report of the Bureau of Ethnology, 1882–1883 (Washington, DC: Smithsonian Institution, 1886); *Aboriginal Pottery of the Eastern United States,* Twentieth Annual Report of the Bureau of American Ethnology, 1898–1899 (Washington, DC: Smithsonian Institution, 1903).

11. Philip Phillips, "Introduction to the Archaeology of the Mississippi Valley" (Ph.D. dissertation, Department of Anthropology, Peabody Museum, Harvard University, 1939).

12. Dumont de Montigny, *Mémoires historiques sur la Louisiane,* edited by Le Mascrier, 2 vols. (Paris, 1753); translation in Holmes, *Aboriginal Pottery,* 57.

13. The following technological and functional discussion is based largely on Michael G. Million, "Ceramic Technology of the Nodena Phase People (ca. A.D. 1400–1700)," *Southeastern Archaeological Conference Bulletin* 18 (1975): 201–208, and a chapter titled "Ceramic Technology" in Vincas Steponaitis, *Ceramics, Chronology, and Community Patterns: An Archeological Study at Moundville* (New York: Academic Press, 1983), 17–45.

14. Sander E. van der Leeuw, "Preliminary Report on the Analysis of Moundville Phase Ceramic Technology," *Southeastern Archaeological Conference Bulletin* 24 (1981): 105–108.

15. See Le Page du Pratz, *Histoire de la Louisiane* (Paris, 1758), vol. 2, p. 179, cited in John

R. Swanton, *Indian Tribes of the Lower Mississippi Valley and Adjacent Coast of the Gulf of Mexico,* Bureau of American Ethnology Bulletin 43 (Washington, DC: Smithsonian Institution, 1911; reprint, New York: Johnson Reprint, 1970), 62.

16. John R. Swanton, *The Indians of the Southeastern United States,* Bureau of American Ethnology Bulletin 137 (Washington, DC: Smithsonian Institution, 1946; reprint, Washington, DC: Smithsonian Institution Press, 1979), 549–554.

17. Philip Phillips and James A. Brown, *Pre-Columbian Shell Engravings from the Craig Mound at Spiro, Oklahoma* (Cambridge, MA: Peabody Museum Press, 1978), 197.

18. Martha Ann Rolingson, "The Toltec (Knapp) Mounds Group in the Nineteenth Century," in *Arkansas Archaeology: Essays in Honor of Dan and Phyllis Morse,* edited by Robert C. Mainfort Jr. and Marvin D. Jeter (Fayetteville: University of Arkansas Press, 1999), 130–133.

19. Phyllis A. Morse, *Parkin: The 1978–1979 Investigation of a Cross County, Arkansas, Site,* Research Series 13 (Fayetteville: Arkansas Archeological Survey, 1981), 20.

20. Phillips, "Archaeological Survey in the Lower Yazoo Basin," 930.

21. Jeffrey P. Brain, "The Archaeological Phase: Ethnographic Fact or Fancy?" in *Archaeological Essays in Honor of Irving B. Rouse,* edited by R. C. Dunnell and E. S. Hall (The Hague: Mouton, 1978), 311–318.

22. Edward Gaylord Bourne, *Narratives of the Career of Hernando de Soto* (New York: Allerton Book Company, 1922), 120–121.

23. Robert C. Dunnell and Martha K. Jackson, "Technology of Late Mississippian Polychromes" (paper presented at the annual meeting of the Southeastern Archaeological Conference, Little Rock, Arkansas, October 1992); Martha K. Jackson, "Pigments on Late Mississippian Polychrome Ceramics from the Central Mississippi Valley" (master's research paper, Department of Anthropology, University of Washington, Seattle, 1993).

24. Roger T. Saucier, *Geomorphology and Quaternary Geologic History of the Lower Mississippi Valley* (Vicksburg, MS: United States Army, Corps of Engineers, Waterways Experiment Station, 1994).

25. Erhard Rostlund, *Freshwater Fish and Fishing in Native North America,* Publications in Geography 9 (Berkeley: University of California, 1952). Rostlund found that the historical freshwater fishery of the lower Mississippi Valley was the second most productive one in North America, after inland Florida.

26. Bruce D. Smith, *Middle Mississippi Exploitation of Animal Populations*, Anthropological Papers 57 (Ann Arbor: Museum of Anthropology, University of Michigan, 1975).

27. Kevin E. Smith, Stephen T. Roger, and Michael C. Moore, personal communication, July 21, 2003.

28. The game called *chunkey,* played by many Southeastern Indian peoples, involved starting a smooth stone roller across a prepared ground, or "chunk yard," and then throwing poles after it with the object of seeing whose pole landed closest to where the stone stopped. See Swanton, *Indians of the Southeastern United States,* 682–684.

29. Phillips, Ford, and Griffin, *Archaeological Survey,* 160–162.

30. Joseph C. Neal, "Birds in Arkansas Prehistory," in Douglas A. James and Joseph C. Neal, *Arkansas Birds: Their Distribution and Abundance* (Fayetteville: University of Arkansas Press, 1986), 49–61.

31. Moore, "Antiquities of the St. Francis," 309–317. Today, Clarence B. Moore's collections are dispersed among many museums and repositories. The bulk of his collections and field notes are in the Smithsonian Institution's collections curation facility in Suitland, Maryland, but significant collections of Moore's vessels are also in the Peabody Museum at Harvard, the R. S. Peabody Museum in Andover, Massachusetts, the Springfield (Massachusetts) Science Museum, the Buffalo (New York) Museum of Science, and the Louisiana State Exhibits Museum, Shreveport.

32. Brandon, "Death and the Parkin Phase," 115–128.

33. Kelly J. Mulvihill, "Neeley's Ferry: Investigations into a Mississippian Fortified Site" (paper presented at the annual meeting of the Southeastern Archaeological Conference, Birmingham, Alabama, November 1996).

34. Phillips, Ford, and Griffin, *Archaeological Survey,* 329–334.

35. Bourne, *Narratives of the Career of Hernando de Soto,* 118.

36. Jeffrey M. Mitchem, "Mississippian Research at Parkin Archeological State Park," in *Proceedings of the Fourteenth Mid–South Archaeological Conference,* edited by Richard Walling, Camille Wharey, and Camille Stanley (Memphis, TN: Panamerican Consultants, 1996), 25–39; Jeffrey M. Mitchem, "Changing Ideas about the Parkin Site, Northeast Arkansas" (paper presented at the annual meeting of the Southeastern Archaeological Conference, Macon, Georgia, November 2000).

37. David W. Benn, "Moon: A Fortified Mississippian–Period Village Site in Arkansas," in *Changing Perspectives on the Archaeology of the Central Mississippi Valley,* edited by Michael J. O'Brien and Robert C. Dunnell (Tuscaloosa: University of Alabama Press, 1998), 225–257; Michael J. O'Brien, *Mississippian Community Organization: The Powers Phase in Southeastern Missouri* (New York: Kluwer Academic/Plenum Publishers, 2001); James E. Price and James B. Griffin, *The Snodgrass Site of the Powers Phase of Southeast Missouri,* Anthropological Papers, vol. 66 (Ann Arbor: Museum of Anthropology, University of Michigan, 1979).

38. John R. Swanton, *Indian Tribes of the Lower Mississippi,* 380–381.

39. Moore, "Antiquities of the St. Francis," 303.

40. One exceptionally large charred post stub was excavated in the summit of the principal mound at Parkin in 1965. It has been suggested that this was the remnant of the huge cross that the Spaniards raised in the summer of 1541 atop "a lofty mound which had been built on a cliff overlooking the river" in the Native town of Casqui. A radiocarbon date on a sample of the post, calibrated to A.D. 1515–1663, indicates that this is at least a possibility. See Mitchem, "Mississippian Research," 37. (The "lofty mound" quotation is from John Grier Varner and Jeannette Johnson Varner, translators and editors, *The Florida of the Inca* [Austin: University of Texas Press, 1951], 432.)

41. By the eighteenth century, most Southeastern Indians had ceased to build and use mounds, but French narratives from the beginning of that century give us glimpses of communities with mounds among the peoples of the lower Mississippi Valley. These writers tell us that in the Grand Village of the Natchez stood two mounds. On one mound was the cabin of the Great Sun, and on the other, a temple holding stone and clay images, a sacred perpetual fire, and cane chests containing the bones of deceased members of the elite Sun lineage. See Swanton, *Indian Tribes of the Lower Mississippi,* 45–256.

42. Mulvihill, "Neeley's Ferry."

43. Additional examples of east Arkansas head vases are illustrated in Holmes, *Aboriginal Pottery,* pl. 43; Moore, "Antiquities of the St. Francis," pl. 15; Clarence Bloomfield Moore, "Some Aboriginal Sites on Mississippi River," *Journal of the Academy of Natural Sciences of Philadelphia,* 2d ser., 14 (1911): pl. 36; Phillips, Ford, and Griffin, *Archaeological Survey,* fig. 111; Hester A. Davis, "An Introduction to Parkin Prehistory," *Arkansas Archeologist* 7 (1966), fig. 3; Lawrence Mills, "Mississippian Head Vases of Arkansas and Missouri," *Missouri Archaeologist* 30 (December 1968): 1–83; Dan F. Morse, ed., *Nodena: An Account of Seventy-five Years of Archeological Investigation in Southeast Mississippi County, Arkansas,* Research Series 4 (Fayetteville: Arkansas Archeological Survey, 1973), cover illustration; and Roy Hathcock, *Ancient Indian Pottery of the Mississippi River Valley*, 2d ed. (Marceline, MO: Wallsworth Publishing Co., 1988), 216–219. Dr. James Cherry, of Fayetteville, Arkansas, has devoted two decades to research on head vases. From museum collections, published references to vessels now unavailable, and private collections, Cherry recorded 135 individual whole or partial head vases (personal communication, August 6, 2002).

44. Early European narratives mention the taking of enemy heads, as well as scalps. Henri de Tonty, second-in-command of LaSalle's 1682 voyage of exploration on the Mississippi River, recorded that in the Tensas village in northeastern Louisiana in 1682, "the temple is surrounded with strong mud walls, in which are fixed spikes, on which they place the heads of

their enemies whom they sacrifice to the sun." Isaac Joslin Cox, ed., *The Journeys of Rene Robert Cavelier, Sieur de La Salle* (New York: Allerton Book Co., 1922), 21.

45. Phillips, Ford, and Griffin, *Archaeological Survey,* 116; John H. House, "Excavations at the Clay Hill and Kent Sites, Lee County, Arkansas," *Arkansas Archeologist* 34 (1995): 35–38.

46. Claude Lévi-Strauss, *Totemism,* translation of *Le totémisme aujourd'hui* by Rodney Needham (Boston: Beacon Press, 1963), 89.

47. James Mooney, *Myths of the Cherokee,* Nineteenth Annual Report of the Bureau of American Ethnology (Washington, DC: Smithsonian Institution, 1900), 316–19, as cited by Charles Hudson, *The Southeastern Indians* (Knoxville: University of Tennessee Press, 1976), 177–178.

48. Mainfort and Demb, "Edwin Curtiss's Archaeological Explorations," 16–17.

49. Frederic Ward Putnam, *Fourteenth Annual Report of the Trustees of the Peabody Museum of American Archaeology and Ethnology* (1881), 20. By "early writers," Putnam was presumably referring to the de Soto entrada chroniclers and perhaps to the writings of early eighteenth-century French visitors to the Natchez. Stephen Williams has pointed out that from the time of Thomas Jefferson and before, it was the consensus among scholars that the Moundbuilders were Indians. See Stephen Williams, "Reviewing Some Late Nineteenth-Century Archaeological Studies: Exploding the Myth of the 'Myth,'" in *Proceedings of the Twenty-first Mid-South Archaeological Conference: Ethnicity in Archaeology,* compiled and edited by C. Andrew Buchner (Memphis, TN: Panamerican Consultants, 2002), 5–19.

50. Jeffrey P. Brain and Philip Phillips, *Shell Gorgets: Styles of the Late Prehistoric and Protohistoric Southeast* (Cambridge, MA: Peabody Museum Press, 1996), 392–394; Vernon J. Knight, "Some Speculations on Mississippian Monsters," in *The Southeastern Ceremonial Complex: Artifacts and Analysis,* edited by Patricia K. Galloway (Lincoln: University of Nebraska Press, 1989), 205–210; Vernon J. Knight Jr., James A. Brown, and George Lankford, "On the Subject Matter of Southeastern Ceremonial Complex Art," *Southeastern Archaeology* 20 (2001): 129–141.

51. Jan F. Simek, Alan Cressler, Charles H. Faulkner, Todd M. Ahlman, Brad Creswell, and Jay D. Franklin, "The Context of Late Prehistoric Cave Art: The Art and Archaeology of Eleventh Unnamed Cave, Tennessee," *Southeastern Archaeology* 20 (2001): 142–153.

52. Henri Joutel, *A Journal of the Last Voyage Perform'd by Monsr. de la Sale* (London, 1714; reprint, New York: Readex Microprint, 1966), 159.

53. Mainfort and Demb, "Edwin Curtiss's Archaeological Explorations," 25.

54. Phillips, Ford, and Griffin, *Archaeological Survey,* 284–290, fig. 75.

55. P. Morse, *Parkin,* 33–43.

56. North American archaeologists reserve the term "arrow points" for the comparatively small—usually less than three centimeters in length—stone projectile points that appear in late prehistory. Often called "bird points" by non-archaeologists, these artifacts tipped arrows that were used in hunting game of all sizes and in war.

57. Dan F. Morse and Phyllis A. Morse, *Archaeology of the Central Mississippi Valley* (New York: Academic Press, 1983), 282–284.

58. Jeffrey M. Mitchem, "Faunal Analysis and Radiocarbon Dates from the Meador Site: ARF-Funded Studies Yield New Insights," *Field Notes: Newsletter of the Arkansas Archeological Society* 300 (May–June 2001): 3–9.

59. To further the University of Arkansas Museum's compliance with NAGPRA, the United States National Park Service in 1995 funded a study of 393 human skeletal remains from the museum's work in the 1930s at the Hazel, Cummings Place, Vernon Paul, Neeley's Ferry, and Barton Ranch sites in the St. Francis region. These analyses augmented results from previous studies of smaller series of human remains from the Parkin and Big Eddy sites; see Brandon, "Death and the Parkin Phase."

60. Brandon, "Death and the Parkin Phase"; Katherine Ann Murray, "Bioarcheology of the Parkin Site" (bachelor of arts honors thesis, University of Arkansas, Fayetteville, 1985); Katherine Ann Murray, "Bioarchaeology of the Post-Contact Mississippi and Arkansas River Valleys, 1500–1700 A.D." (master's thesis, Department of Anthropology, University of Arkansas, Fayetteville, 1989); Jerome C. Rose and Anna M. Harmon, "Bioarcheology of the Louisiana and Arkansas Study Area," in *Archeology and Bioarcheology of the Lower Mississippi Valley and Trans-Mississippi South in Arkansas and Missouri,* edited by Marvin D. Jeter, Jerome C. Rose, G. Ishmael Williams Jr., and Anna M. Harmon, Research Series 37 (Fayetteville: Arkansas Archeological Survey, 1989).

61. Putnam, *Fourteenth Annual Report,* 12.

62. Ibid.

63. Jon D. Muller, "Structural Studies of Art Styles," in *The Visual Arts, Plastic and Graphic,* edited by J. Cordwell (The Hague: Mouton, 1979), 139–211.

64. Vincas P. Steponaitis, M. James Blackman, and Hector Neff, "Large-Scale Patterns in the Chemical Composition of Mississippian Pottery," *American Antiquity* 61 (1996): 555–572.

65. Robert C. Mainfort Jr., "The Late Prehistoric and Protohistoric Periods in the Central Mississippi Valley," in *Societies in Eclipse: Archaeology of the Eastern Woodland Indians, A.D. 1400–1700,* edited by David S. Brose, C. Wesley Cowen, and Robert C. Mainfort Jr. (Washington, DC: Smithsonian Institution Press, 2001), 173–189.

66. Henry F. Dobyns, *Their Number Become Thinned: Native American Population Dynamics in Eastern North America* (Knoxville: University of Tennessee Press, 1983); George F. Milner, "Epidemic Disease in the Postcontact Southeast: A Reappraisal," *Midcontinental Journal of Archaeology* 5 (1980): 39–56; Ann F. Ramenofsky, *Vectors of Death: The Archaeology of European Contact* (Albuquerque: University of New Mexico Press, 1987).

67. David W. Stahle, Malcom K. Cleaveland, and J. G. Hehr, "A 450-Year Drought Reconstruction for Arkansas, United States," *Nature* 316, no. 6028 (1985): 530–532.

68. David S. Brose, "Introduction to Eastern North America at the Dawn of European Colonization," in *Societies in Eclipse: Archaeology of the Eastern Woodland Indians, A.D. 1400–1700,* edited by David S. Brose, C. Wesley Cowen, and Robert C. Mainfort Jr. (Washington, DC: Smithsonian Institution Press, 2001), 1–7.

SUGGESTED READING

Brain, Jeffrey P., and Philip Phillips

1996   *Shell Gorgets: Styles of the Late Prehistoric and Protohistoric Southeast.* Cambridge, MA: Peabody Museum Press.

Brain and Phillips assembled and compared data on hundreds of engraved shell gorgets and stylistically similar artwork in other media from the Southeast. Examining the stratigraphic context and archaeological associations of these materials at Moundville, Alabama, and elsewhere, they suggested a controversial chronology for pan-Southeastern art styles.

Browman, David L., and Stephen Williams, editors

2002   *New Perspectives on the Origins of Americanist Archaeology.* Tuscaloosa: University of Alabama Press.

The various contributors to this book present the fruits of manuscript and archival research on topics such as colonial-era deductions and speculations about American Indian origins, European influences on nineteenth-century American archaeology, and early work by women archaeologists. A number of the essays highlight the career and contributions of Frederic Ward Putnam.

Galloway, Patricia K., editor

1989   *The Southeastern Ceremonial Complex: Artifacts and Analysis.* Lincoln: University of Nebraska Press.

In 1984, L. B. Jones, of Minter City, Mississippi, convened a conference at the Cottonlandia Museum in nearby Greenwood that brought together professional and amateur archaeologists and collectors to share ideas about a complex of interrelated, prehistoric, pan-Southeastern art styles. This book grew out of the Cottonlandia conference. Its essays cover topics ranging from artifacts in their regional context to interpretations of prehistoric iconography in light of historic and modern Native American belief systems. The volume also includes an illustrated catalogue of hundreds of artistically noteworthy artifacts from across the Southeast that were exhibited at the conference. It offers something for everyone.

Hudson, Charles

1976   *The Southeastern Indians.* Knoxville: University of Tennessee Press.

This ethnological introduction to Indians in the Southeast—peoples such as the Cherokee, Creek, Choctaw, Chickasaw, Natchez, Seminole, and Yuchi—has become a classic. Hudson's treatment of cultural themes, highly innovative at the time, leads off with "Belief System" and proceeds to discussions of social organization, subsistence, art, and recreation. The book ends with the sobering account "A Conquered People."

Jeter, Marvin D.

1990   *Edward Palmer's Arkansaw Mounds.* Fayetteville: University of Arkansas Press.

With primary documents and extensive background essays, Jeter tells the colorful story of Curtiss's contemporary, the naturalist Edward Palmer, who was recruited by the Smithsonian Institution to explore Indian mounds in Arkansas in 1881–1884. The volume reproduces drawings by African American artist Henry Jackson Lewis, whom Palmer employed to illustrate mounds and excavations.

Mainfort, Robert C. Jr., and Sarah R. Demb

2001   "Edwin Curtiss's Archaeological Explorations along the St. Francis River, Northeast Arkansas, 1879–1880." *Arkansas Archeologist* 41: 1–27.

Mainfort and Demb rescue Edwin Curtiss from obscurity by painstakingly transcribing and presenting his Arkansas documents in their entirety and reconstructing the chronology and itinerary of his expedition on the St. Francis River.

Moore, Clarence Bloomfield

1910   "Antiquities of the St. Francis, White and Black Rivers, Arkansas." *Journal of the Academy of Natural Science of Philadelphia,* 2d ser., 14: 255–364.

1911   "Some Aboriginal Sites on Mississippi River." *Journal of the Academy of Natural Sciences of Philadelphia,* 2d ser., 14: 367–468.

In these two reports, reproduced together with others in a single journal volume, Moore described the results of collecting expeditions he conducted during two successive winters along the "interior" St. Francis, White, and Black Rivers and along the Mississippi River proper. Generations of archaeologists have mined Moore's publications for their wealth of archaeological detail, but they are beloved foremost for their beautiful color lithographs of artifacts. Comparison of the vessels Moore found along the St. Francis with those found a year later along the Mississippi highlights the cultural distinctiveness of the two regions.

1998   *The Lower Mississippi Valley Expeditions of Clarence Bloomfield Moore.* Edited and with an introduction by Dan F. Morse and Phyllis A. Morse. Tuscaloosa: University of Alabama Press.

Eastern North American archaeologists are grateful to the University of Alabama Press for this and other volumes in the recent series of C. B. Moore reprints. Readers who have access to long-established research libraries, however, will want to consult the original publications for the sake of the color lithographs.

Morse, Dan F., and Phyllis A. Morse

1983   *Archaeology of the Central Mississippi Valley.* New York: Academic Press.

This is a detailed but highly readable summary of regional archaeology by two archaeologists who spent three decades conducting research in northeastern

Arkansas. The authors emphasize material culture, environmental adaptation, and cultural dynamics over twelve thousand years of history and prehistory. The book includes many illustrations of artifacts and sites.

Morse, Phyllis A.
1981   *Parkin: The 1978–1979 Investigation of a Cross County, Arkansas, Site.* Research Series 13. Fayetteville: Arkansas Archeological Survey.

This slim, unpretentious volume reports one of the most fully realized studies to come out of the 1970s–era settlement pattern archaeology.

Muller, Jon D.
1997   *Mississippian Political Economy.* New York: Plenum Press.

Muller uses the theoretical perspective of historical materialism to refocus scholarly discussion of prehistoric Mississippian culture on the empirical data of archaeology and ethnohistory. This highly original—even controversial—book is rich in detail on evidence for demography, technology, production, social organization, and exchange in Mississippian society.

O'Brien, Michael J., and Robert C. Dunnell, editors
1998   *Changing Perspectives on the Archaeology of the Central Mississippi Valley.* Tuscaloosa: University of Alabama Press.

Essays by fourteen contemporary authors present innovative and, for the most part, scientifically oriented studies of prehistoric archaeology in the central Mississippi Valley.

Phillips, Philip, and James A. Brown
1978   *Pre-Columbian Shell Engravings from the Craig Mound at Spiro, Oklahoma.* Cambridge, MA: Peabody Museum Press.

Depression-era commercial "mining" of a late prehistoric burial mound on the western periphery of the Mississippian world produced an enormous corpus of elaborately engraved marine shell objects. Phillips and Brown pursued the widely dispersed Spiro engraved shell artifacts and recorded them in a series of rubbings that then formed the core of their massive analysis, which weds art history with archaeology.

Phillips, Philip, James A. Ford, and James B. Griffin

1951   *Archaeological Survey in the Lower Mississippi Alluvial Valley, 1940–1947.* Papers of the Peabody Museum of American Archaeology and Ethnology 25. Cambridge, MA: Harvard University. Reissued, with a new introduction by Stephen Williams, by the University of Alabama Press, Tuscaloosa, 2003.

The "Phillips, Ford, and Griffin" volume is a perennial classic of American archaeology. Contemporary readers—and not just professionals and graduate students—will appreciate the lucid exposition of the distinctive and complex Mississippi Valley environment, a candid and occasionally humorous discussion of methods of artifact classification, and the subtle repartee among the three authors.

Swanton, John R.

1946   *The Indians of the Southeastern United States.* Bureau of American Ethnology Bulletin 137. Washington, DC: Smithsonian Institution. Reprint, Washington, DC: Smithsonian Institution Press, 1979.

John R. Swanton was the foremost scholar of Southeastern Indian ethnology of his day and perhaps of all time. His encyclopedic compendium catalogued contemporary and historic tribes of the Southeast (many of the former now resident in Oklahoma) and presented a thematic treatment of Southeastern Indian culture richly supported by excerpts from often obscure early historical sources.